The
GREATEST
LESSON

I'VE EVER LEARNED

Bill Bright was a Southern California businessman and agnostic when, through a series of events in the late 1940s, he sensed that there indeed was a God who loved him and had a special plan for his life. Bright studied five years at Princeton and Fuller Theological Seminaries, then resigned his business and founded Campus Crusade for Christ International on the UCLA campus with his wife, Vonette. Campus Crusade has since grown into a multi-faceted, multi-national ministry with more than 16,000 full-time and associate staff serving around the world. During the 1990s, one of the organization's major emphases will be New Life 2000, a cooperative strategy involving thousands of ministries, churches and individuals to present the gospel of Jesus Christ around the world.

Early in his ministry, Bright compiled key Scriptures into a booklet to help people understand how they could trust Jesus Christ as Savior and Lord. The booklet, titled "Have You Heard of the Four Spiritual Laws?" has since become one of the most widely-used ministry tools in existence, with more than one billion copies in print in scores of languages.

Bill Bright has also authored several books, including *Witnessing Without Fear, The Secret,* and *Promises: A Daily Guide to Supernatural Living.* Recently he and Vonette collaborated on a book for "couples on the fast track," *Managing Stress in Marriage.*

All royalties from the sale of the men's volume of *The Greatest Lesson I've Ever Learned* are being donated to the planting of the New Life 2000 training centers in Moscow and Leningrad, and to support the continuing ministry of "JESUS" film teams in the Soviet Union.

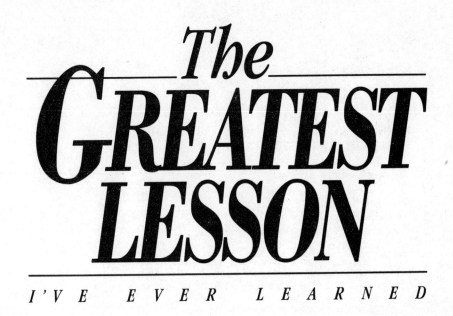

The GREATEST LESSON

I'VE EVER LEARNED

Bill Bright

EDITOR

Here's Life Publishers

First Printing, June 1991

Published by
HERE'S LIFE PUBLISHERS, INC.
P. O. Box 1576
San Bernardino, CA 92402

Library of Congress Cataloging-in-Publication Data
The greatest lesson I've ever learned / Bill Bright, editor.
   p.   cm.
   ISBN 0-89840-332-4
   1. Christian biography—United States. 2. Men—United States—
Biography. 3. Men—Religious life. 4. Christian life—Anecdotes.
I. Bright, Bill.
BR1700.2.G75   1991
209'.2'2—dc20
[B]   91-16458
                                 CIP

Cover design by David Marty Design

For More Information, Write:
L.I.F.E.—P.O. Box A399, Sydney South 2000, Australia
Campus Crusade for Christ of Canada—Box 300, Vancouver, B.C., V6C 2X3, Canada
Campus Crusade for Christ—Pearl Assurance House, 4 Temple Row, Birmingham, B2 5HG, England
Lay Institute for Evangelism—P.O. Box 8786, Auckland 3, New Zealand
Campus Crusade for Christ—P.O. Box 240, Raffles City Post Office, Singapore 9117
Great Commission Movement of Nigeria—P.O. Box 500, Jos, Plateau State Nigeria, West Africa
Campus Crusade for Christ International—Arrowhead Springs, San Bernardino, CA 92414, U.S.A.

Contents

I would like to express my special thanks and deep gratitude to my dear friends who have been open and honest in sharing their challenging and heartwarming greatest lessons to make this remarkable book possible; to Dan Benson of Here's Life Publishers who suggested the idea for the book; to my editorial director Don Tanner and his staff, Joette Whims, Greg Kriefall and Mary Taylor, who coordinated the project and assisted in the editorial process; and to my beloved wife Vonette, who is a constant encouragement to me.

To
the Reader

While reading *The Greatest Lesson I've Ever Learned,* written by many well-known women and edited by my wife Vonette, I was genuinely moved. Their heartwarming stories, in which they shared their "greatest lessons" of how God had become a reality in their lives, ministered to me deeply.

Suddenly it occurred to me that I should edit a similar book for men. I sent a memo to the publisher only to discover that Dan Benson, the vice president and editorial director, had sent me a similar memo which crossed mine in the mail.

So I invited a number of dear friends whom I greatly admire and whom God is using in special ways to join me in this project. Although not all of them could participate for good and valid reasons, I am deeply grateful to those who did. My heart has sung praises to God again and again as I have read the testimonies of these men whose stories you are about to read. In the process, I also have shed tears and laughed a lot.

As I was writing and editing the introductions of each author, I found myself expressing my love and appreciation for each one in such phrases as "he has a special place in my heart" or "he is a beloved friend" or "he is very dear to me." Finally, it occurred to me that after reading a few chapters you would, no doubt, have good reason to question my sincerity. Therefore, I have chosen to express my deep love and profound appreciation to and for each one in this introduction.

I am confident that you will enjoy and greatly benefit from reading each contribution as I have. To benefit the most from your reading, ask God to help you respond to the lessons these men have learned. Open your heart to the joy and the pain they have so generously shared.

Thousands of Christians have found the women's version of *The Greatest Lesson* to be an ideal gift for every occasion. If you have not discovered the book, you may want to send copies of both books to your friends and acquaintances.

This book can be a tool to share meaningful and heartwarming stories with those who need encouragement. *The Greatest Lesson* can be a powerful witness to the men in your life and can draw them closer to our Savior.

Bill Armstrong

<hr>

People Really Want to Know

For many years, Senator William Armstrong has been one of the most articulate legislators in Washington. During his distinguished political career, Bill was admired by both friend and foe for his integrity and knowledge of the issues. He served in the Colorado House of Representatives, the Colorado Senate, and the U.S. House of Representatives before his election to the U.S. Senate in 1978.

I met Bill and Ellen at a small dinner party hosted by another congressman who arranged the meeting to communicate the gospel to his congressional colleagues. Few men in the secular world have had such a powerful witness for our Lord, as many thousands have come into the kingdom through Bill's anointed communication of the gospel.

THE GREATEST LESSON...

Now retired from office, Bill plans to devote even more time to evangelism and to his media business. In his stirring account, he shares with us his deep desire to introduce his neighbors and friends to the love of Christ.

"I have done something so terrible, I do not see how God could ever forgive me," the young woman told me.

It was a startling disclosure and all the more so because of the circumstances. She had come to visit me in my office in the U.S. Senate. And her admission took me totally by surprise because this was a woman with a sunny disposition and a winning smile. She had a good job and many friends. In short, she was someone with few cares as far as I could see.

But her manner was unusually serious as she told me of her concern, and then she asked me one of the most significant questions I have ever encountered. "I have heard that you have a personal relationship with God. Could you tell me how I could have such a relationship?"

I didn't have to think twice. Referring to a little pamphlet called *The Four Spiritual Laws*,* I quickly explained God's plan of salvation.

"Law One: God loves you and offers a wonderful plan for your life.

---

* I relied on *The Four Spiritual Laws* with great confidence, having used this effective ministry tool on many previous occasions. This litte tract was instrumental in my own conversion a number of years earlier. Since then, I have quoted the "laws" (really the distilled essence of the New Testament) in hundreds of speeches and personal conversations. Instead of shrouding the gospel in complex and forbidding verbiage, this pamphlet is simple and direct. In my opinion, it is divinely inspired and the best ministry tool of its kind of which I am aware.

"Law Two: Man is sinful and separated from God. Thus he cannot know and experience God's love and plan for his life.

"Law Three: Jesus Christ is God's only provision for man's sin. Through Him you can know and experience God's love and plan for your life.

"Law Four: We must individually receive Jesus Christ as Savior and Lord. Then we can know and experience God's love and plan for our lives."

I briefly elaborated on each of these points and explained that each is drawn directly from the Bible. Then after a few minutes of discussion, I assured my young friend that, if she wished to do so, she could receive Jesus Christ as her personal Savior. According to the Bible, several things would instantly happen: Her sins would be forgiven; she would be assured of eternal life in heaven with God, the Father, and with his Son, Jesus; and in this life, she could aspire to peace, joy, gentleness, self control and much, much more.

She prayed the little prayer suggested in the booklet: "Lord Jesus, I need You. I open the door of my life and receive You as my Savior and Lord. Thank You for forgiving my sins. Take control of the throne of my life. Make me the kind of person You want me to be."

She departed realizing that her life was changed forever and that God had wonderful plans for her. As you can imagine, I considered it a high privilege to be able to share the Good News in this way. How great God is to have made it possible!

But it wasn't until some time later that I recognized the unusual aspect of our meeting. We had talked about Christ and prayed together. But I had often done so previously. What was remarkable was this young lady's presence of mind and poise to ask such an intelligent and

13

direct question: "How can I have a personal relationship with God?"

It finally occurred to me that perhaps many people have the same question but are too embarrassed to ask. Or don't know whom to ask. Or feel that they have to purify themselves before approaching God. Or think that extensive study is required. Or have some other opinion that obscures the simplicity and love of Jesus Christ.

As I thought it over and began to look around me more carefully, it became obvious that there are many people, some of them hoping desperately for significance and meaning in their lives, who simply do not have the clarity of thought to ask directly, "How can I have a personal relationship with God?"

I have tried to become more sensitive to people around me. As I have done so, it has become clear that most people will rarely ask directly for spiritual help unless someone else begins the conversation or, in some way, gives them an opening to do so.

I have discovered that there are people all around us—in our offices, the schools we attend or where we teach, on airplanes, in service clubs, possibly even in our own churches or among our own families—who would love to know God but do not know how to ask or are too embarrassed to ask. Many are tormented by guilt or distracted by the false notion that God wants them to suffer.

Even those who are in dire circumstances—contemplating severe illness, financial problems, addiction, divorce or even suicide—usually do not know how to ask for help in the intelligent and direct manner of the young woman in my office. Hindered by lack of experience, embarrassment or misunderstanding, they silently try to cope alone.

Interestingly, however, the vast majority of people I have come in contact with are willing, often eager, to discuss

14

spiritual issues if someone else will break the ice. And, if given an opportunity to do so, a high percentage of those hearing the gospel will respond.

In the last fifteen years or so, I have had the privilege of speaking personally with many people about Jesus Christ, often using *The Four Spiritual Laws* as the basis for discussion. A few have responded indifferently; a tiny number have been hostile; but thousands have listened with an open mind to what Jesus promises and have received Him as their personal Savior.

Even those who were not ready to personally accept Christ have often expressed appreciation that someone cared enough about them to explain how to have a personal relationship with God. I can only assume that in many cases they wished to reflect further and, subsequently, made a life-changing decision.

One young couple in Washington comes to mind. A member of the U.S. House of Representatives and his wife attended a dinner party in a fashionable Capital neighborhood. Dr. Bill Bright spoke informally about how to become a Christian. This young congressman and his wife listened courteously but without visible reaction. But I learned later what happened. After hearing the brief explanation of how to become Christians, this rising young political couple went to their own home, knelt down in their bedroom, and received Christ as they prayed. In the years since, they have become a role model of Christian family life and have, themselves, led thousands to Christ.

So I have learned a great lesson. I do not have to go to a third world country to be a missionary or to the inner city or to some other place I instinctively think of as a missionary field. One of the greatest missionary opportunities in the world is in my own neighborhood, my own home and my own place of work.

15

People we encounter every day are longing to find answers to life's major questions: Who am I? Where did I come from? What's life all about? Is there a God? Is there life after death? People are eager, often desperate, for someone to explain how their lives can be significant and meaningful. And while most will not initiate a conversation about Jesus, they almost always are open to discussing Him if someone else gets the conversation started.

What a noble opportunity—to introduce our friends, our business and professional colleagues, people in our neighborhood, even our own family, to the One who promises forgiveness of sin, eternal life, the right to become a child of God, and much, much more.

I have also learned that the best opportunities often arise in completely secular settings. Frankly, most of those who need to hear the gospel will never come to church. But we meet them every day in our offices, clubs and schools, in airports and restaurants. Jesus lived among every-day people, just as we do. He spoke to them of life-and-death issues in mundane settings—over meals, while traveling, in the country, in cities. He did not wait for people to come to Him. He went to them. And we have the extraordinary privilege of following His example.

Pat
Boone

What Do You Say
to a Jewish
Pornographer?

Pat Boone has been in the entertainment business since his teenage years in Tennessee, when he won a spot on the Ted Mack Amateur Hour. Since that time, he has sold more than 45 million records.

Not only is Pat an accomplished singer, but he is also an author, actor and television performer. He is the author of The Miracle of Prayer, *a reprint of the popular* Pray to Win.

I have observed Pat closely through the years and know him to be a true ambassador for our Savior. He has championed many wonderful causes on behalf of our Lord and

17

country. For the past several years, he has been the national chairman and host of the Easter Seal Society telethon, and co-chairman of the National Day of Prayer.

Pat relates an intriguing story of his encounter with a pornographer in Las Vegas in which Pat learned how much God personally loves each of us.

"Hey, Boone, I read your book!"

I cringed.

Normally, I'm delighted to know the Lord has provided another opportunity for me to share my story.

But—a *Jewish pornographer?*

In the steam room at the Sands Hotel?

In Las Vegas?

I sensed a punch line coming and braced myself for it. But none came. The squat, curly-haired man whose current business was selling pornographic material and grotesque sex machines was looking at me earnestly.

"You're serious about this, aren't you?"

I nodded, still apprehensive. "Sure I am. Where in the world did you get hold of my book?"

"From Frankie Avalon." (I had given several copies to entertainer friends, including Frankie, Dean Martin, Bob Goulet, and Johnnie Ray—but *not* to anybody I thought might find it "weird" or just joke material, like Ace here. I guess he'd be the *last* guy in Las Vegas I'd have shared my story with—and now we stood dripping and steaming together, with several friends looking on in disbelief.)

"I'd like you to pray for me," Ace said softly.

18

I guess everybody's jaws dropped, including mine. Was this guy joking? Was he setting me up for something?

"I mean it. I always thought this religion stuff of yours was some kind of phony trip, just part of your 'image'—you know. But the book really got to me.

"Look, I know why my life is so messed up. I'm my own worst enemy. I've been married four times, bankrupt twice, and if I knew some other way to make a living, I wouldn't be selling this junk. I sure ain't proud of it.

"I'm fat, flabby and over forty, and now the doc tells me I've got to go in for a gall bladder operation—and I'm scared to death. I'd really like you to pray for me."

I could swear I felt goose bumps in that 170-degree heat!

"Look, Ace," I said, not daring to glance at the other guys, "I'll be happy to pray for you. I will. But you know, God wants to hear from *you* about your problems. That's really the whole idea. Will you pray, too?"

The look on his face seemed a mixture of sadness and hilarity, if you can imagine such a thing. The twin forces rushed together and erupted into a loud laugh, "Me? *Pray?* Oh, come on! God would strike me dead, tell me to get lost or go to hell, or something! You gotta be kidding!"

I sensed a real loneliness, a vacuum in this man, and suddenly saw the hard, gruff exterior for what it was—a disguise.

"Ace," I said, obeying an inner impulse before I quite realized how rash it was, "so many people have the wrong idea about prayer and about God Himself. He's not interested in just hearing religious words from so-called religious people. Jesus Himself said there was only one really *good* person—and that was God! So God wants to hear from each one of us, not because we're good, but because He just plain ol' *loves* us!

19

"Look, I didn't arrange for you to read my book. I would have tried to keep it *away* from you, figuring you wouldn't dig it at all. So God must have wanted you to read it and made it possible. He knows your heart a whole lot better than I do, and I know now He'll hear and answer your prayer.

"Tell you what—I've never suggested this to anybody, but I'm going to pray that *God will be real to you in some way that you'll recognize!* I don't know what He'll do, but I believe He'll show you in some way that He hears you, and that you're getting through. Will you pray for the same thing?"

"I don't know how to pray, Boone—I really don't." Ace looked a little uneasy, suddenly aware of the unbelieving stares of the others.

"I don't mean right here, now," I said, "but later, when you're alone. You don't have any trouble talking to *me*, do you?"

Ace grinned, a little relieved maybe. "No—but you're not God!"

"That's right, I'm not! But you can talk to Him just like you're talking to me. The words just don't matter because He's listening to your heart anyway. It's important, though, that *you* speak to Him. Will you do it?"

"Okay. I'll try it, but—I don't know." He shook his head, and we walked out of the steam room.

On the way down to the hotel where I was working, I talked to the Lord out loud, "Dear Jesus, I don't know what I've gotten us into, but I really do pray for Ace. And I do pray right now that You'll show him—*in some way he'll recognize*—that You're listening to his prayer. Will You do it—please? Thank You, Lord."

It sounds good now when I tell it, but I confess that my faith was pretty shaky. A Jew? A pornographer? A wild

20

Las Vegas character—what had I gotten the Lord and me into? Or was it just me?

I prayed a lot for Ace the next two days.

I didn't see him, and I wasn't sure I wanted to.

But my engagement had come down to its final night, and for one last time, I went back to the Sands Health Club for a good steam and massage. I imagined I'd see Ace—and was sort of nervous about it.

He wasn't there. But while I was sitting in the steam room, the attendant pushed open the door to tell me I was wanted on the phone—a guy named Ace. As I went to pick up the receiver, I couldn't help wondering if I'd been set up for an elaborate joke, and this was the punch line.

The excitement on the other end of the line quickly erased the thought. "Your prayers are *answered!* YOUR PRAYERS ARE ANSWERED!" The voice was so loud I had to hold the phone away from my ear.

"Hold on, Ace," I squeezed the words in edgewise. "What happened? What do you mean?"

"Boone! You know you said to just talk to God like I was talking to you? And to ask Him to show me something? Well, I thought you were probably crazy, but I did it. I mean, I talked right out loud, like you said. I really felt like I was talking to the lamp or the air, and I didn't think my words were gettin' outta the room—but I did it."

"And you must have been praying too—right?"

I chuckled. "I sure was!"

"Well, *lemme tell you what happened!*

"I went in today for my last examination before the gall bladder operation. I was scared to death. The doc gave me this chalky stuff to drink and then X-rayed me. In a little while he came in with the X-rays just shaking his head—he

21

said he *couldn't find the stones! The gallstones are gone!* The doc says he can't operate on me when he can't find the stones!"

I was numb. "That's fantastic, Ace!"

"Yeah—but what do I do now?"

Again, I was practically speechless. I said the first thing that came to my mind. "Well, Ace, the main thing is—don't look at this as the end of anything, just the beginning!"

"Yeah . . . ?" He was eager. He wanted more.

"Why don't you get yourself a Bible and start reading about the One who's done this for you? It's obvious that He loves you, Ace. I'm amazed myself—but you know now that He's listening to you, don't you?"

Ace interrupted, "Yeah. Yeah! I can dig it!" And he hung up!

He was running somewhere to get a Bible!

And there I sat, my mouth full of "Buts" and "Waits," my brain full of directions for him, my heart wanting to urge him into a good church fellowship—and my hand full of dead phone.

Slowly, as I sat there, I began to see how much God loved this "former" pornographer—and I realized Ace was in good hands.

God loves every last one of us—*equally.* And *He knows which ones are ready to respond* to His miraculous touch. We don't. If all the people in Las Vegas had lined up for me to talk and pray with, I'd have asked Ace to stand at the end of the line.

God put him at the *very* front.

The God of miracles cares about each of us personally! And because He's supernatural and miraculous in His very nature, a personal relationship with Him will invariably produce miracles in anyone's life.

What is a "miracle?" *The touch of God in your life.* I purposely chose this simple, all encompassing definition because I have discovered that God uses many means to change things for us. It may *seem* natural, but if it has God's fingerprints on it, it's a miracle! And life becomes very exciting.

Does this God touch your life through the chaos and uncertainty of our crumbling world? Then respond! It's a miracle! God Himself, in His gentle, loving concern for you, is cutting across the laws of nature and science—for you!

I've never seen Ace again. He ran to get a Bible, and I didn't get to tell him anything more. Lord, You sure love him, don't You? Well, please don't let him get away.

And Ace, wherever you are—God loves you.

Tony
Campolo

Ordinary People
Who Do
Extraordinary Things

A professor of sociology at Eastern College, Dr. Tony Campolo is a popular author and lecturer.

Tony's deep conviction that Christians should be in the forefront of social issues is reflected in his activism. He developed Cornerstone Christian Academy, a school for inner-city children with learning difficulties. He also founded an organization to establish hospices for AIDS victims under Christian auspices. He is a member of the international board of directors of Habitat for Humanity.

Tony has a great love for Christ and a desire to introduce Him to others. I view Tony as a superb and effective spokesman for our Savior and asked him to participate in this book because of my warm affection and high esteem for him.

Here Tony recalls the exciting Saturday night he spent as a youngster in a youth group called the "Bible Buzzards." These teens were led by an ordinary man who demonstrated an extraordinary caring. His humorous account of how anyone can be used of God to reach others for Christ will certainly encourage you to share the Good News with those around you.

When I was fifteen years old, a friend of mine, Burt Newman, invited me to go with him to a Bible study on a Saturday evening. I had grown up in church and thought I knew all the basic stuff that a teenager was supposed to know about Christianity. But none of it had stirred me sufficiently to make me want to go to a Bible study on a Saturday night.

Saturday nights were for fun, and so far as I was concerned, studying the Bible was a boring thing that people did at Sunday school to earn Brownie points with God. But Burt was a good friend. So for his sake I went.

At 7:30 on the dot, we arrived at the small row house where this Bible study was supposed to happen. Walking through the front door, I was surprised to see that the place was jammed with teenagers. They were sitting on every available inch of floor and were packed together on every step of the stairway. Finding myself an inconspicuous place to sit underneath the dining room table, I quickly joined in with this hyper gang of teenagers and was soon enjoying a solid hour of gospel singing.

The whole thing seemed corny to me. The songs were

25

all too familiar. I had learned them in Daily Vacation Bible School. Choruses like *Do Lord* and *I'm Traveling on the Hallelujah Line* were typical of the selections. Even so, I was enjoying myself. I especially liked the constant joking around and the good-natured verbal jabbing that went on between songs—most of it surprisingly clever, and all of it had us laughing.

At 8:30 it was time for the actual Bible study to begin. Everyone but me whipped out a Bible and turned to the Book of Ephesians. I could see that these kids were serious. I really had never seen such earnestness about Bible study before.

The teacher was a thin, almost gaunt, man who wore a seemingly pencilled mustache. He was hardly charismatic in personality and definitely not what I was expecting. Later I learned that he earned his living as an accountant, and upon reflection, I could have guessed the same just by looking at him. He fit every stereotypical image of an accountant.

Crouched under the dining room table, I listened intently as Tom Roop read and expounded on two verses in the second chapter of Ephesians. He didn't tell any jokes. His message was not very scholarly. But I sensed something special about him. At first I couldn't put my finger on it. But after several weeks, I figured out what it was about him that kept more than forty teenagers totally rivetted on what he had to say.

It was that he cared. That was it! He *really* cared. He cared about us, and he cared about the Bible, and he cared that we all knew what the Bible was about. He believed that theology was important and that we were smart enough to understand what was wrapped up in that Pauline epistle. Going to that Bible study became a ritual every Saturday night all during my high school years.

The ridiculous name which these bright-eyed teenagers adopted certainly reflected the kind of group we were. We called ourselves the *Bible Buzzards!* Every time I mention that name, it always draws incredulous smiles. Mr. Roop thought the name appropriate because he saw us as young people who had ravenous desires to "devour the word of truth."

But before you laugh at us too quickly, consider some of those who attended the meetings: *George Fuller,* who would become an outstanding Bible scholar and eventually the president of Westminster Theological Seminary; *Keith Harman,* who would earn his doctorate and teach religion at Ursinus College; *Bob White,* who would become academic dean of Duke University; *Preston Ramson,* who would win the Tennessee Williams Playwright Award for his play *King Crab,* which was a hit on Broadway and PBS television. Besides them, at least fifteen pastors came out of that group who have faithfully brought a host of persons to Christ. And then there's my friend Burt. He is now the professor of pastoral care at the Episcopal Seminary in Alexandria, Virginia.

The story of Tom Roop is the account of what extraordinary things an ordinary layman can do for Christ. What he accomplished demonstrates how *caring* makes the difference. Even to this day, Mr. Roop keeps in touch with "his kids" and regularly prays for them. What else would you expect? From Tom Roop, I learned that "lay" Christians have a special calling to spread the gospel.

This lesson was reinforced one day on a flight I took from Philadelphia to Orlando, Florida. I was on my way to a Christian festival where it would be my privilege to speak to more than twenty thousand people. I was feeling pretty smug about myself. *After all,* I thought, *I am going to be used by God in a mighty way.*

Sitting in my window seat, I happened to look across the aisle. Settled next to the window on the opposite side of the plane was a stunningly attractive woman. At about the time I saw her, I noticed a New Yorker who had just gotten on the plane sauntering down the isle. Don't ask me how I knew he was from New York. I knew! He was wearing a blue satin shirt open almost down to the waist so he could show off his hairy chest. Two heavy gold chains hung lazily around his neck. And as he approached, I knew where he would sit. Regardless of where he had been assigned, there was no doubt in my mind but that he would sit next to the beautiful woman who had just caught my eye.

I was right!

Over the next few minutes, his moves were a wonder to behold. He smoothly engaged her in conversation. This man definitely knew what he was doing; he had gone through this line before. But just as soon as the conversation seemed to be getting intense, I watched her reach into her purse and whip out a Bible. The incongruity forced me to work hard to keep from laughing.

All the way to Orlando, this wonderful young woman explained the way of salvation to her new friend, showing him from Scripture what Jesus had done for him on the cross and what he had to do to be "saved."

When the plane landed and pulled up to the gate, almost everyone stood as soon as possible to disembark— everyone, that is, except the New Yorker and the woman. Both had their heads bowed in prayer as they asked Jesus to become a saving presence in the man's life.

When I think of Tom Roop and of that young woman, I remember that God builds His kingdom primarily through ordinary people who are willing to use daily encounters to tell others about the salvation which is available in Jesus Christ.

Televangelists have their place. Revivalists call a lot of people to Christ. And I suppose that Christian books also have a contribution to make in the evangelistic task commissioned by our Lord. But in the final analysis, it seems clear that most people are won to Christ by ordinary lay persons who, in almost unnoticed ways, love people into the kingdom of God and who, at some risk, use their daily encounters with strangers as opportunities to witness for Christ.

Charles Colson

———◇———◇————

My Cancer and the Good-Health Gospel

Having served seven months in federal prison for a Watergate-related offense, former presidential aide Chuck Colson saw first-hand the tremendous obstacles facing prisoners, ex-prisoners and their families. In 1976 following his release from prison, Chuck founded Prison Fellowship, a Christian outreach to inmates behind and beyond prison walls.

As chairman of the board of Prison Fellowship, he ministers regularly in prisons across the country and around the world. Recognizing that America's overcrowded prisons are failing to rehabilitate offenders, Chuck often speaks out for reform of existing criminal justice practices.

Chuck has become a friend whose intellect and warm

30

heart yielded to our Lord has made him one of the most popular speakers and writers of our generation. He is always an inspiration and a blessing to me.

Chuck writes a monthly column for Christianity Today *and contributes regularly to numerous newspapers and magazines. He is the author of several books, including* Born Again, Kingdoms in Conflict, The God of Stones and Spiders, *and* Loving God.

Through his bout with cancer, Chuck found new purpose for the trials Christians suffer. His experience will inspire you to view your suffering in a new light also.

Coming out of the anesthesia, I first saw the smiling faces of my wife Patty and daughter Emily. "Did they get it all?" I asked. Patty gripped my hand. "Yes."

"Was it malignant?"

Emily nodded. "Yes, Daddy—it was cancer. But they got it all, and you're going to be okay."

Cancer.

I had always wondered, in secret fear, what it would be like to be told I had cancer. I thought I would be shattered. But I had prayed for the grace to withstand whatever the doctors found. And, as many have discovered before me, I saw in the confrontation with fear and suffering that there is nothing for which God does not pour out His grace abundantly. I felt total peace—and great thankfulness that a merciful God had brought me to that recovery room.

My stomach problems began in November 1986 during a ministry trip to the Philippines. I flew home. My doctor told me that I was badly run-down, that I had a bleeding ulcer, and to stay away from airports for a while. With rest and proper diet, the problem was soon cured.

Just when my stomach seemed fine, I talked with a dear Christian brother, Dr. Joe Bailey of Austin, Texas. Joe urged me, as my own internist had already done, to have a gastroscopy. The idea of inhaling a tube so doctors could view the scenery inside my stomach was not particularly inviting. Besides, the ulcer had already healed. But Joe kept insisting.

So I submitted to the horrors of the gastroscope. The doctor told me, as I had expected, that the ulcer was gone. Then came the unexpected: He had discovered a tumor in my stomach lining.

After weeks of additional tests, experts concluded the growth was benign. There was no reason to hurry to have it removed. Once again Joe Bailey called. "Chuck," he said in his Texas drawl, "get that thing out, and get it out as quick as you can."

"I can't! I'm writing a new book. I have ministry commitments, speaking obligations."

But Joe would not be moved. And since by then I suspected that God was speaking through him, I scheduled the operation for early January.

To everyone's surprise, the tumor was a low-grade malignancy. Because it was caught early, however, doctors have assured me my prognosis is excellent. If it had gone undetected, the outcome could have been far different. The previous fall's nagging ulcer served as a warning by which God got my attention—and then he used Joe Bailey's stubborn concern to get me into the hospital.

God's grace provided not only peace and protection, but new purpose. I had, as some friends know, begun to burn out from too many writing, speaking, and ministry commitments.

But as I lay in my hospital bed, I thought through my real priorities. Had I unconsciously boarded the evangelical treadmill? Trying to do all those worthy things that everybody wanted me to do, had I become beholden to a tyrannical schedule rather than to God's will? Several weeks tied to hospital tubes is a good time to reflect on the larger perspective of God's design in our lives.

My suffering provided some fresh insights as well into the health-and-wealth gospel. If God really delivers His people from all pain and illness, as is so often claimed, why was I so sick? Had my faith become weak? Had I fallen from favor?

No. I had always recognized such teaching as false theology. But after four weeks in a maximum-care unit, I came to see the good-health gospel as something else: a presumptuous stumbling-block to real evangelism.

During my nightly walks through the hospital corridors dragging an I.V. pole behind me, I often met an Indian man whose two-year-old son had endured failed kidney transplants, a brain aneurysm, and was now blind for life.

When the father, a Hindu, discovered I was a Christian, he asked if God would heal his son if he, too, was born again. He said he had heard things like that on television.

As I listened, I realized how arrogant health-and-wealth religion sounds to suffering families: Christians can all be spared suffering, but little Hindu children go blind. One couldn't blame a Hindu or Muslim or agnostic for resenting, even hating, such a God.

I told my Hindu friend about Jesus. Yes, He may miraculously intervene in our lives. But we come to God not because of what He may do to spare us suffering, but because Christ is Truth. What He does promise us is much more—the forgiveness of sin and eternal life. I left the hospital with my friend studying Christian literature, the Bible, and my own account in *Born Again*. If he becomes a Christian, it won't be on false pretenses.

I thought often in the hospital of the words of Florida pastor Steve Brown. Steve says that every time a non-Christian gets cancer, God allows a Christian to get cancer as well—so the world can see the difference. I prayed I might be so filled with God's grace that the world might see the difference.

Steve's words represent a powerful truth. God does not witness to the world by taking His people out of suffering, but rather by demonstrating His grace through them in the midst of pain.

He allows such weakness to reveal His strength in adversity. His own Son experienced brokenness—and died—that we might be freed from the power of death. But we are promised no freedom from suffering until we are beyond the grave.

Thus, I can only believe that God allowed my cancer for a purpose—just as He allows far more horrific and deadly cancers in fellow Christians every day. We don't begin to know all the reasons why. But we do know that our suffering and weakness can be an opportunity to witness to the world of the amazing grace of God at work through us.

* * *

Editor's note: Colson's surgery was successful, and he has had no recurrence of cancer.

Paul Crouch

Parting the Sea of Impossibility

Paul Crouch began his career in radio and television in 1954 on the campus of Central Bible Institute and Seminary. Since that time, he has moved through a variety of broadcast experiences.

He founded the Trinity Broadcasting Network (TBN) in 1973, and the following year purchased its first television station KLXA-TV, which later became KTBN Channel 40. Under Paul's direction, TBN has become the largest group owner of broadcast television stations in the world.

I am especially drawn to Paul because of his deep love for our Lord and his vision to use his expertise in electronic media to help take the gospel of our Savior to the entire world.

Paul and his wife, Jan, appear together regularly on

the TBN Network. The account of how Paul and Jan and their co-workers struggled to begin a television ministry and how he learned to let God "part the sea of impossibility" will inspire you to greater faith in our Lord also.

When we began our Christian television ministry, the initial stages were like scaling a cliff with only a thin rope between life and death. If the rope didn't hold or our hands lost their grip, all would be lost!

Everything we owned was at stake. We had agreed to pay Bill Myers, the station owner, $10,000 a month for air time. And Jan and I had invested $20,000, which was our life savings, into the new ministry to build the sets, pay the utility deposits, install the phones, rent some TV equipment, and buy the TV time. But after only the third day on the air, our funds were nearly exhausted.

Mr. Myers did not believe in credit, so he demanded an additional $3,000 before he would sign the station back on the air that night. I remember turning to a co-worker and saying, "Now what do we do?" We prayed for God's direction, and in just a few minutes our pastor, Syvelle Phillips, a vital partner in ministry, walked in the door. We explained our predicament to him and asked if he would speak to Mr. Myers. He did and after a lengthy discussion and the payment of our very last $1,000, Mr. Myers agreed to sign the station on that night.

My emotions were so drained after that meeting, I knew it would be impossible for me to face the TV cameras that night. Pastor Phillips said, "Paul, it is time to tell the people our need." He agreed to host the program in my place, and I went home to pray. As I drove toward home, I again

36

began to cry out my complaint to the Lord. "Why does it have to be so hard, Lord? Why do we have to suffer so much? Lord, You have provided everything we have needed up to now—what does this all mean?"

As I wept before the Lord, a still small voice spoke sweetly to me—so clearly that it startled me. The Lord said, "Paul, it is difficult because you have not *given* Me anything."

The message startled me even more. "What do you mean, Lord? I have given you everything—my job at KHOF, my life, my talents, *even* our $20,000 savings!"

The Lord spoke again: "You did not *give Me* your savings, you *loaned* them to Me."

Yes, it was true! The Lord knows everything—even our thoughts. I had taken a note back for the money Jan and I had placed in the ministry. We had only loaned God the money.

God was sayng, "I want you to *give* Me your savings." For me this was an awesome request. Didn't God know how Jan and I had sacrificed for sixteen years to save this money? Didn't He know we had gone without to put this money away for our future? But money had become a hindrance to my spiritual growth—perhaps even a god, of sorts, and the Lord was asking me to give it up—all of it!

I struggled with the decision all the way home, and finally as I fell across the bed, I conceded, "All right, God, I will make a bargain with You. If You will cause Your people to give an equal amount tonight on television, I promise I will give it *all* to you!"

I picked up the phone and called the station. By now a full-fledged telethon was underway. Pastor Phillips was pouring out his heart to the people, telling of our need at TBN. It seemed that an unusual anointing of the Holy Spirit was upon him as he and his co-host spoke of our vision to reach fourteen million people in Southern California with the gospel.

Somehow I reached Jan, who was helping on the telephones. I said, "Honey, God has spoken again." I told her what I had promised the Lord. Then I said, "Tell Pastor Phillips that a pledge for $20,000 has come in from a man who loves the Lord and believes in Christian television very much—if God's people will match it with an equal amount tonight."

There was a long pause an the other end of the phone as Jan began to weep softly. She knew better than anyone the struggle raging within my soul. My mind was in such turmoil by then, I don't remember all that was said between us, but I do remember Jan's last words over the phone: "I love you . . . "and she was gone.

In a moment I watched as Jan, tears streaming down her face, slipped onto the TV set beside Pastor Phillips and gave him the message. The challenge was given and the phones began to ring and ring and ring . . .

In less than one hour, God's people had not only matched the challenge, but had given a $10,000 surplus!

After only three nights on the air—on a station which had been silent for six months—God spoke to His people to give more than $50,000. And since the need was so urgent, dozens of God's beautiful people drove to the studio and personally delivered the gifts to "their" TV station. All praise to His Wonderful Name! The "Red Sea" of impossibility had parted, and we were walking across on dry ground!

One of the pledges from that first telethon came from a most unusual source. A little missionary couple, Robin and Marva Farnsworth, had just returned from New Guinea on furlough. They had been working for eight years in the most primitive, disease-and-mosquito-infested jungles of the world as Bible translators with Wycliffe. The privation and physical pain they and their three children had endured would fill a book, and the evidence was clearly written on their drawn faces.

Brother Farnsworth met me at the door of TBN the next day. "Paul, God has spoken to me, and I am giving you the balance of our travel fund for your new TV ministry." He held out a check with trembling hand. "God will supply our needs, I know. Please take it with our love."

My heart nearly burst within me as I saw this thin little man with the scars of spiritual and physical battle upon him standing before me, asking to minister and give to my need. Tears welled up in my eyes as I opened the check—it was for $1,480. "Oh, Brother Farnsworth, no! I cannot take your travel funds!"

A look of intense physical pain rushed over his face. His voice was almost stern as he pressed the check into my hand. "Paul, God told me to do this; I have to obey the Lord! You *have* to take it!"

Through experiences like these, I have learned one of my greatest lessons in life: God will part the sea of impossibility if we are willing to give our all for Him.

If you ever wonder why God is blessing TBN, look back at the precious seed which has been planted by faithful servants of God who gave sacrificially like the Farnsworths. They beautifully exemplify the principle in Psalm 126:6: "He that goeth forth and weepeth, bearing precious seed shall doubtless come again with rejoicing bringing his sheaves with him" (KJV).

God is worthy of all that we are and have and is faithful to complete His plan in and through our lives. This missionary family has already proven this. Though they are back in the jungles of New Guinea, they are rejoicing and sharing in the reward of thousands of souls who have accepted Jesus as Savior since TBN began!

Ted DeMoss

Sitting on
the Sidelines
While God Works

Ted DeMoss is an outstanding businessman who has worked in the insurance business for many years. At one time, he had nineteen offices in five states with more than a hundred salesmen.

One of the most popular speakers for the Christian Business Men's Committee of USA, Ted has averaged more than 100,000 miles of travel a year for more than thirty years. He was president of CBMC for more than fourteen years and presently serves on their national board.

I have known, loved and respected Ted for many years. He is a layman who has inspired tens of thousands of other laymen to seek first the kingdom of God and to be faithful witnesses for our Savior. He is the author of the book, The Gospel and the Briefcase.

Ted describes a humorous and tender experience as a young insurance salesman that changed his life dramatically and started him on an adventure of bringing Christ's message of love and forgiveness to many others.

In the course of my job selling insurance, I walked into an apartment building one day to call on a man whose name had been sent to my office in response to a direct mail program. I went to the door of his third-floor apartment and knocked.

The man inside spoke through the door without opening it, "Who's out there?"

I had learned that in selling insurance you never say, "the insurance man," because people might not open the door. So I just replied cheerfully, "I'm Ted DeMoss . . . "

I'm one of those fellows who received Jesus Christ and soon afterward became convinced of the greatest lie ever perpetrated on Christians by Satan: There are two kinds of Christians in the world, the full-time worker and the rest of us. I thought my job was to make money and put it in the offering plate, thus allowing the preacher, missionary and evangelist to win the world to Christ. No one ever told me that they were supposed to be the coaches and we the players in this great contest for the souls of men.

When I was in my mid-twenties, I became involved with a local Christian Business Men's Committee (CBMC). There for the first time, I met men who were committed to sharing their faith in Jesus Christ. They believed their responsibility was to help fulfill the Great Commission of our Lord in which He said, "Go into all the world and preach the Good News to everyone, everywhere" (Mark 16:15, TLB).

At first I was skeptical. I even remembered seeing the body of my college professor who had taken his life some years before and the anger within me because no preacher had reached him with the gospel message. Yet, as a Christian, I had actually taught under this scholar for a year and had never sensed any responsibility to share Christ with him. As I became more involved with CBMC, I was encouraged to start praying for men who did not know Jesus Christ and, as the Holy Spirit directed, to share the Good News with them as a way of life. This meant talking to them about Christ one on one, bringing them to a CBMC luncheon or dinner where a lay speaker would give his testimony, or inviting them to my home for dinner to tell them about Jesus Christ.

Through CBMC I learned that as long as I was usable and available, the Holy Spirit would show me when I was supposed to speak to someone. I started to pray that, sometime before I died, the Lord would let me see just one person commit his life to Christ as a result of my sharing the Good News with him.

So as I stood outside the door of that third-floor apartment and answered, "I'm Ted DeMoss," I was ready for such an opportunity.

The man inside bristled defensively. "If I open this door, I'll throw you down those stairs. Now get away from my door!"

Since I sincerely thought that he had inquired about insurance, I persisted. "Mister, I'm not going to hurt you. Please open the door. I've got to talk to you."

I fully intended to talk with the man about insurance, but when he opened the door, I realized there was no point

42

in that. Before me stood a man with a white beard who looked like a thin Santa Claus. I hadn't been in the business long, but I knew he was too old to buy any insurance I might sell him. Looking directly at me, he demanded, "I opened the door. Now, what do you want to talk about?"

"I want to come in and talk to you."

"What do you want to talk about?" he snapped.

I persisted. "May I come in?"

As I spoke, the Spirit of God impressed me to talk with this man, a complete stranger, about Jesus Christ. At age twenty-five, I had never done that before.

Finally, he stepped aside and said, "Come in, then."

I entered, and we both sat down on the couch in the living room. Looking straight at me, the elderly man asked curiously, "What do you want to talk about?"

I paused just for a moment, then said the only thing that came to mind. "I want to read the Bible to you."

Talk about no training in witnessing for Christ! I had absolutely no preparation apart from what my CBMC friends had told me about reading the third chapter of John.

"Go ahead," he consented.

"I don't have a Bible," I said weakly. "Do you have a one?"

He looked puzzled for a moment. "I don't know whether I have a Bible or not. I've been blind for many years."

I asked if I could look around the apartment for one, and he agreed. After a brief search, I found a Bible covered with dust on top of a stack of books.

Walking back to the couch, I opened the Bible to the third chapter of John and began to read slowly. The further I read, the more scared I felt. My friends at CBMC had never

43

told me what to do next. So I read slower and more deliberately until I got to verse 18:

> He that believeth in him is not condemned: but he that believeth not is condemned already, because he hath not believed in the name of the only begotten Son of God (KJV).

I finished that verse, praying silently for the Lord to give me wisdom as to what I should do. I looked over at the old man, and what I saw shocked me—his beard was wet with tears! God had indeed spoken to this man through His Word.

"Sir, would you like to invite Jesus Christ into your life right now, right here?" I asked softly.

The man nodded thoughtfully, "Well . . . I would like to do it right now, but not here."

"Where do you want to do it?"

"I want to do it with my mother."

Mentally, I was scratching my head. The man had told me he was eighty-one, and I thought, *What do I say now?*

I decided to ask, "Where is your mother?"

"In the kitchen," he pointed.

Thinking he had a picture of her hanging in the kitchen, I supposed he wanted to go there for sentimental reasons. We made our way back to the kitchen, and to my surprise, there was his mother sitting in a canvas-backed chair. She was ninety-eight years old and an invalid.

I can still hear the man's words as if he were speaking them today: "Mother, God has sent a man to our home."

I had gone on this call thinking the insurance company had sent me, but I quickly realized that what he was saying was true.

"He's been reading the Bible to me, and I'm going to accept Jesus Christ."

I have never heard anyone scream like she did in my life! When she regained control of her emotions, the aged woman said an amazing thing: "Mister, I don't know who you are, but I have prayed for my boy every day for over eighty years."

Her son and I got on our knees, and I had the joy of praying with him and seeing him come to Christ. God had answered two prayers: hers of eighty years, and mine of just a few weeks.

In the Bible, I had read that some plant, some water, and God gives the increase (1 Corinthians 3:6). I had been there to participate in the increase. The man's faithful mother and a Christian man on the first floor of the building had done the planting and watering. The neighbor, I learned, had been taking care of their physical needs for several years. He would come up every day and get their grocery order, find out what other needs they had, and take care of them. He had often shared Christ with the blind man.

I was so excited that I didn't work the rest of the day. My wife Edith was a registered nurse at the hospital on the 11 P.M. to 7 A.M. shift. I had to tell her what had happened, so I drove home and woke her up. I spoke enthusiastically of how God had answered my prayer and had given me the joy of seeing a person find Christ even though I didn't know much about sharing my faith. "Honey, I've found a reason for living as a Christian—something I can give my life to, and that is *people!*"

I went back to visit the man once before Edith and I moved to Chattanooga, Tennessee, later that year. It is amazing—when I try to think of other events that happened in 1951, I can't remember anything more significant than this experience! It changed the course of my life.

THE GREATEST LESSON...

Can you imagine a person coming to Christ the first time you ever tried to witness? I guess our Lord knew I might never try again had I been rebuffed. The Holy Spirit prepared the old man's heart and convinced him to accept Jesus. He just let me sit on the sidelines and watch as He worked. And I've been doing it ever since!

James
Dobson

Surrendering
My Expectations
and Ambitions

The founder and president of Focus on the Family, Dr.
James Dobson is a leading authority on the family.

Jim is one of the most respected and honored leaders
in the Christian world. His commitment to building strong
families has brought blessing to millions of people. And
because of his expertise on family matters, he was invited
regularly to the White House to consult with President
Ronald Reagan and his staff and more recently with President
George Bush.

Jim is the distinguished author of eleven bestselling
books, including Dare to Discipline *which has sold more*

than two million copies and was selected as one of fifty books to be rebound and placed in the White House Library.

Jim's dramatic account of his struggle to let God control and bless his work and ministry can help each of us learn how to turn our ambitions over to Him also.

I've spent most of my professional life writing and speaking about person-to-person relationships of one kind or another. So it may be surprising to hear that one of the most important lessons I've had to learn had to do with the way I relate to people—specifically, the way I respond to them on paper!

Let me explain.

I am a writer. I've always expressed my thoughts best in written language. Even when I was ten years old, I would write letters to my parents if I thought they had disciplined me unfairly. I much preferred to make my case on paper than face to face.

Through the years, therefore, my first reaction when I was irritated was to express that sentiment in writing. It was not until about 1981 that I began to see the disadvantages of that approach. There are many.

First, *when words are put on paper, their intensity does not diminish with the passage of time.* There in the files, or at home in a spouse's possession, is a fiery message that carries its original impact even years after everyone has forgotten the issue that motivated it. When angry thoughts are expressed in black and white, they remain alive and dangerous—like an armed pipe bomb!

Second, *there is something powerful about the written*

48

language. Remember that Jesus identified Himself entirely with the Scriptures: "In the beginning was the Word, and the Word was with God, and the Word was God" (John 1:1, NKJ). Even the words of man can be a two-edged sword that cuts the soul to the quick. Harsh, spoken words can also be destructive, of course, but they can't compare to those that are carefully arranged on paper and served piping hot.

Third, *I found that my tendency to put my reprimands in writing set the stage for other members of my staff to do the same.* They began criticizing one another in memo-form, which brought immediate retaliation and counter charges. I quickly realized this was wrong.

Fourth, *I discovered that my face-to-face encounters with those who needed correcting were not nearly so severe or painful.* Sometimes the person was able to give me a logical explanation that I hadn't considered. On other occasions, I saw vulnerability in his or her eyes that softened my own irritation.

What I'm trying to say is that the Lord began talking to me about this entire area, and I have mellowed significantly in recent years. But the criticism of harshness some have leveled at me has certainly been valid in times past. I was never capricious or vicious to people as a matter of course. Most of my strong memos went to those who deliberately or slovenly failed to meet a need or follow a well-known policy. I have never been a tyrant to work for. Still, I needed to make some significant changes in the way I related to my colleagues—and I've attempted to do that.

As you might expect, this tendency to be tough, especially in writing, has applied to my relationship with business associates outside Focus on the Family, too. As a matter of fact, it was in this area that the Lord hit me between the eyes with one of the strongest, most direct warnings I've ever received from Him on this subject.

As I've grown older and a bit wiser, I have actually felt constrained to go back to the publishers of some of my early books and ask forgiveness for the things I demanded of them. I'll never forget the time when my second book, *Hide or Seek*, came out. It arrived on the heels of *Dare to Discipline*, which had been enormously successful. I did not want to be a flash in the pan—a one-book author—who had nothing else of importance to say. As a result, I felt a great deal of pressure to produce another bestseller. It was carnal pride, pure and simple.

For some reason, I found *Hide or Seek* difficult to write, and I bogged down for two years in the process. It is probably my favorite book now, but I went through a tough time giving birth to it. When the book finally came off the press, I was one uptight young author. I was determined to make it go, or else. I went to New York City in 1974 and participated in seventeen radio, television, and newspaper interviews within a span of only three days. No price was too great to let the world know the book was available.

Shortly thereafter, Ernie Owen, my publisher from Fleming H. Revell in New Jersey, came to see me at Children's Hospital. We went to eat together, and I gave him fits during lunch.

"How come I can't find copies of *Hide or Seek* in the Christian bookstores?" I demanded. "Where are you advertising the book, and why are you not keeping me informed of your plans?"

On and on I went. Suddenly, the man who is now my good friend fired his own shots at me.

"I want to know something about *you*," Ernie said firmly. "How come this book is so important to you? Why are you acting like this? Why are you so uptight about the job we are doing?"

Ernie probably didn't know it at the time, but his

50

responses made me furious. Instead of doing his job as my representative, I believed he was being rude to me and making me feel foolish for insisting on quality work from my publishers.

I quickly finished eating, shook hands with Ernie, and headed across the street to the hospital. I got about fifty yards from the restaurant when the Lord spoke to me. It was not an audible voice, but it was unmistakably His!

He said, "Son, those questions that Ernie was asking you a few minutes ago did not originate with him. They came from Me. I also want to know why you are pushing and shoving everyone so hard. Tell Me why you're trying to force this book to be a success. Don't you know that you have nothing but what I have given you and that *Hide or Seek* will be successful only if I choose to bless it? So why are you trying to promote it on your own?"

If you have ever been "spanked" by the Lord, you know it is an unpleasant experience. I felt about three feet high.

"I understand, Lord," I said humbly and released *Hide or Seek* into His hands. "It is Yours. If You can use it, that's fine, and if not, I surrender my personal ambitions."

Hide or Seek took off like a rocket that month and is still selling well seventeen years later.

My point is that I am an intense person with strong opinions about how things ought to be done. I was especially that way when I was younger. I also had a pretty powerful temper in those days. But the Lord is beating those characteristics out of me. If I can live another hundred years, I may turn out to be a pretty nice guy!

51

Steve Douglass

Redeeming Those Drifting Moments

For more than twenty-two years, it has been my privilege and delight to work closely with Dr. Steve Douglass as a fellow staff member of Campus Crusade for Christ where he now serves as our executive vice president.

Steve is a man of God with a brilliant mind and a vision for helping to change the world for the glory of God. He is in great demand as a speaker on leadership, management and various biblical topics and has been used to introduce many thousands of students and executives to Christ through his speaking and personal ministry.

Steve graduated with highest honors from Massachusetts Institute of Technology and Harvard Graduate School of Business Administration. He is the author or coauthor of several books including Managing Yourself, How to Get Better Grades and Have More Fun *and* Enjoying Your Walk With God.

Here Steve reveals his secret to a supernatural walk with God even when circumstances don't go his way.

The elderly lady stepped off the small commuter plane and started walking in my direction. She was angry. She was greeted by a woman standing near me—her daughter—who hadn't seen her for some time. The mother continued to grumble and fume, so I couldn't help but hear.

It seems that she was led to believe that her commuter flight gate in LosAngeles International Airport was just a hundred yards away and, in fact, it proved to be 150-200 yards.

Yes, that was it. She had to walk another hundred yards and apparently hated every step of it. By now she had meditated on that for two hours and had worked herself into quite a stew.

That incident led me to learn a crucial spiritual lesson. Like this lady's mind, my mind also has almost a life of its own. Something goes wrong and it's off to the races. Before long, I can be concerned and even upset at a level far beyond what the original circumstance warranted.

How does that work? Well, over time, my mind adds fuel to the fire. It brings to memory other things the offending person has done. It projects future conversations I might have with that person and guesses that he might say further unkind things in such a dialog. It supplies other reasons why I shouldn't like that person.

Before long, I have mentally "tried and convicted" that person of "crimes" he has never and will likely never commit. What is as bad is that I am experiencing real and present anxiety over my fabricated storyline.

So what did I discover was the cure to this persistent mental malady? *Displacement*—pushing the fabrication out of my mind with a reality even more true than the original bad event.

What is displacement? It occurs when one thing pushes another out of place. For example, when two automobiles try to occupy the same spot in an intersection at the same time, we witness physical displacement; an accident in which one of the cars often ends up pushed out of the way.

So it is with our minds and hearts. Two different sets of thoughts cannot easily occupy the same mind at the same time. Like the elderly lady on the commuter plane, a single concern can enlarge and totally occupy a mind until it becomes unaware and insensitive to the needs of people around it. In her case, she wasn't even civil to her daughter who, I imagine, was expecting a warm and loving reunion.

That is the bad side of our human tendency to be preoccupied. But there is a good side—a way to harness the tendency. I have discovered I can become "preoccupied" with God. And when I do, my thoughts of Him displace my usual concerns.

King David discovered this truth long before I did: "I have set the Lord continually before me; because He is at my right hand, I will not be shaken. Therefore my heart is glad, and my glory rejoices; my flesh also will dwell securely" (Psalm 16:8,9, NASB).

David learned to keep a consciousness of the Lord *continually* in his mind. The word "continually" in Hebrew is *tamid*, which means "without interruption." In other words, David was in a constant sense of the presence of God and probably in a fairly continuous conversation with Him.

What was the impact of his conscious closeness to God? Peace and joy.

And it wasn't that David had no problems. Look at Psalm 16:1: "Preserve me, O God, for I take refuge in Thee" (NASB).

His mind was filled with the reality of the presence of the all-powerful creator-God. From that perspective, David's problems must have seemed very manageable—apparently not even worth worrying about.

I have found the same thing to be true. When I focus my mind on God, pray to Him, cast my cares on Him, even just stay in touch with Him, my normal concerns are pushed right out of my mind. They seem puny compared to God.

So how does this work in practice? The secret is in the implementation. The displacement seems to occur only when I keep the Lord *continually* before me.

The average person thinks on one specific thing for only about eleven seconds at a time. My mind frequently illustrates this statistic. I drift from one thought to another. Oh, I may come back fairly quickly to the main subject on my mind, but even when I am fairly focused, I will drift momentarily to listen to or look at something around me or to pursue a spurious thought.

Redeeming those drifting moments has been the key to setting the Lord before me. When I drift, I try to "let my first stop be God." Most everything I think about can easily be related to and discussed with God in some way. I can thank Him, cast a concern on Him, pray for His provision or solution, or in some other way talk to Him about it.

So my momentary departure from my train of thought can become a wonderful stimulus to talk to God, as opposed to a launching pad for preoccupation with a distracting concern.

Sometimes I find it helpful to be reminded to keep up this habit. When I look down at my wedding ring, I can be reminded not only of my relationship with Judy, my wife, but also of my relationship with God. I ask, "How many minutes has it been since I last talked to God?" If it has been very long, I may well pause right then, sit back and restart my dialog with the Lord.

Does this really work? Let me close with an illustration of how powerfully a continuous walk with God can affect my attitude.

A number of years ago I was having lunch with a friend of mine. When his wife came to the table with her tray of food, the only available seat was to my left. She sat there.

As I talked with my friend, I practiced "letting my first stop be God." Whenever my mind drifted, I talked to God. It was brief. I didn't bow my head, close my eyes or fold my hands. I just directed my thoughts to God for a moment and then returned mentally to the conversation with my friend.

I hardly noticed when his wife got up and returned with a styrofoam cup of hot water for tea. She set it on my side of her tray. The tea bag and stirrer were still in the cup. She suddenly turned to say something to me, and she tipped over the cup of hot water, dumping it entirely onto my leg. Not a drop splashed on her. (Life isn't always fair.)

What did I do? You would think that I'd have cried out in pain and jumped up, right? Wrong! I laughed.

"That's weird," you say.

True, that's weird.

"That's not natural," you add.

True—it's supernatural.

56

STEVE DOUGLASS

You see, it was a long distance from the presence of God to my leg. My mind was elsewhere. My peace and joy were being supplied supernaturally. So it took a while for the pain from my leg to penetrate into my conscious thoughts.

In the words of the song, "The things of earth will grow strangely dim in the light of His glory and grace."

Ted W. Engstrom

Sound Advice, Well Taken

The former president and chief executive officer of World Vision (and now president emeritus), Dr. Ted Engstrom is one of the most influential leaders in American religion and social service.

A prolific editor and author, Ted has written hundreds of articles and more than forty books, including the bestsellers The Making of a Christian Leader, The Fine Art of Mentoring *and* Managing Your Time.

Ted is a giant among men, with whom I have had the joyful privilege of being associated for many years. Among his many other responsibilities, he also serves as chairman of the International Committee of Reference for our worldwide evangelistic effort called New Life 2000.[1] The committee will consist of 1,000 Christian leaders who will serve as centers of influence for this comprehensive global strategy to help reach the world for Christ.

I have admired and respected Ted for his management and writing skills, his sensitivity to the needs and hurts of men and his warm, loving heart for God.

Ted tells how he learned the value of good advice and how listening to counsel from others has affected his life and ministry.

After more than fifty years of serving the Lord, I am constantly amazed at the results of heeding the sound bits of advice given to me as a young boy and as a young man just starting on a career path.

The first good advice which significantly influenced my life came to me from my mother when I was only eight or nine years of age. Although she had completed only eight years of schooling, she was a wise woman.

One day she said, "Ted, I want to introduce you to some of the greatest friends you can ever know. Come with me."

Taking me by hand, she led me to the East Cleveland, Ohio, Public Library where she helped me get my first library card. That day we picked out the first two books—apart from my school books—that I had the joy of reading: *Heidi* and *Black Beauty*. At that moment I was introduced to "friends" who have stood me in marvelous stead over the years.

That incident started me out on a career path I have followed for these many years. I fell in love with books; they have fascinated me. For more than five decades of ministry,

I have read an average of at least one book per week and written more than two score.

The second piece of sound advice came years later when, as a nineteen-year-old college freshman, I received the Lord Jesus Christ as my Savior and Lord. Shortly after that dramatic and dynamic experience, a young college friend suggested that I select a "life verse." Some days later, while reading avidly from God's Word, Psalm 32:8 popped off the page into my heart. God said to me, "I will instruct you and teach you in the way you should go; I will guide you with My eye" (NKJ).

Immediately, I felt that this was the verse God wanted me to claim for my life. I have clung to its assurance of guidance and direction over the years as a drowning sailor might cling to a raft. I have written this verse after my autograph in Bibles and books an untold number of times. And as a constant reminder of God's faithfulness, I have a calligraphy of this beautiful promise hanging on the wall in my study. As a result, I am convinced that every Christian ought to have his or her life verse!

Not long after, another marvelous suggestion came to me from a young Christian friend. He said, "Ted, begin your day with the emphasis of Romans 12:1,2." Here the apostle Paul reminds us, "Present your bodies a living sacrifice, holy, acceptable to God, which is your reasonable service. And do not be conformed to this world, but be transformed by the renewing of your mind, that you may prove what is that good and acceptable and perfect will of God" (NKJ).

This friend explained, "Begin every day by offering your life, walk and ways to the Lord as a living sacrifice. Put your body, mind, will, time, energy and all that you have into the hands of the Lord. Make it a daily experience."

What a wonderful bit of advice this has been. I have

found that God is faithful to tie the promise to guide me in my life verse into this injunction to offer my life to God for His direction.

The final bit of cherished advice came from a man who was to be my beloved father-in-law. My wife Dorothy and I were college sweethearts. A year or so after graduation, I asked her father for her hand. Shortly afterward, he offered me a share in his successful watch-making and jewelry busi-ness. Since Dorothy was his only child, he would train me in the business and turn it over to me in due time.

Reflecting upon this generous offer, I realized that my heart could not be in that kind of business and, though I deeply appreciated his generosity, I explained that my fingers were thumbs and I would not be a good watchmaker nor a capable storekeeper!

Breathing a sigh of relief, he gave me marvelously sound advice. He said, "Son, I'm glad you feel that the Lord is leading you in a specific direction, not necessarily into business with me. As you move on into your career, whatever you do, make yourself as close to indispensable as possible. Strive for this level of performance and excellence in your service for God."

I've never forgotten his wisdom. And I have learned over the years that, when we accept such advice, often un-sought, we are greatly benefited. I have fallen in love with books; the Lord has given me the assurance of His guidance; I have learned the lesson of daily submission to the will of God; and I have sought excellence in my performance. All of this is a result of good advice given and heeded, and I have found these helpful gems to be among "the greatest lessons I have ever learned."

Paul
Eshleman

He Will Provide

Paul and Kathy Eshleman have been a vital part of my life and the ministry of Campus Crusade for Christ for almost twenty-five years. Since joining staff, Paul has assumed major responsibilities and has completed each with remarkable success.

He directed Explo '72 in Dallas, Texas, which brought 85,000 students and laymen to the city for training in how to share their faith in Jesus Christ. Paul also directed the "I Found It" campaign in 1976 which spread to 245 major cities and thousands of smaller communities.

Forty-five years ago, God impressed me to produce a film on the life of Jesus to help accelerate the spread of the gospel to the world. Paul has played a major role in helping to make that dream a reality. In 1978 he was named executive vice president of the Genesis project which produced the "JESUS" film for Campus Crusade. Under his exceptional *leadership, the film has been translated into more than 180 languages and, at this writing, has been viewed by almost 450 million people worldwide—one-twelfth of the world's population. No doubt, tens of millions of these have already received Christ.*

In 1983 Paul served as program director for the International Conference for Itinerant Evangelists in Amsterdam, an event sponsored by the Billy Graham Evangelistic Association. Currently, Paul continues to direct the "JESUS" Film Project and also serves as coordinator of New Life 2000.

In his story, Paul describes how the plans for the huge Explo '72 conference in Dallas almost collapsed and shows how God led him to the right contacts at the right time to pull all the details together.

The starting date for the Explo '72 conference I was directing was less than thirty days away. Every hotel, motel, school, and campground within sixty miles of Dallas was filled to capacity. We had already assigned housing to 50,000 people, but still the registrations poured in at more than one thousand a day.

"We now have over 20,000 people registered who don't have rooms," the registration coordinator told me. "What are we going to do?"

"How about the students going door-to-door asking for places for the delegates to stay? How are they doing?" I inquired.

"They're finding about one hundred places a day. But each day we get further behind."

Concerned about the problem, I decided to call Bill Bright. As president of Campus Crusade for Christ, he had assigned to me the task of preparing for this giant congress. At that time, his office was in Arrowhead Springs, California.

"Bill," I began frankly, "you sent me down here to Dallas to get things ready. You should know that right now I'm not doing a very good job."

"I'll catch the next plane to Dallas," he said after I explained the situation to him.

When he arrived from the airport, I gave him my desk, and we studied the problem.

"Has the Lord given you any ideas of what to do?" he asked.

"Our best idea at this point is to rent empty warehouses and equip them with cots and portable toilets." I suggested. "If you could help us find about 40,000 cots, we could hopefully give everyone a place to sleep."

Immediately, Bill went to work. He called the office of the Secretary of Defense. He talked to the officials in Civil Defense. He even spoke to the President's personal assistant in Washington. Although nothing was confirmed, there seemed to be some hope of a few cots. "Let me know if there is anything else I can do and how this all goes. I'll be praying." And he flew back to California.

Two days later all of the government agencies turned us down because of various policy issues. We didn't get one cot. Even Bill Bright—the president of the organization— hadn't been able to solve the problem. It was time to get on our knees again.

A few of us gathered in my office to pray. In the quiet of my heart, I remembered the words of a speaker I had heard early in my Christian ministry: "If God calls you to a task, He will supply all your needs." Many of this man's talks were based on the example of Nehemiah, whom God told to return

64

to Jerusalem and rebuild the wall of the city. And God provided all that Nehemiah needed by touching the heart of the king who gave him the materials necessary to complete the task.

I had great confidence that God had led us to hold this conference. Already we had seen wonderful answers to prayer in other areas of the project. But this problem was so big—and serious.

I knew that lack of housing could cause everything to come to a halt. If that happened, we would have to write people and tell them not to come. I felt so discouraged.

But as we prayed, I remembered again that I was in God's service. This was not *my* conference. Whatever He wanted would be fine with me.

"Lord, we don't know what to do," I prayed earnestly, "but You do. Show us what to do. You have always supplied our needs. We ask you to do it once again—for Your glory."

As we prayed, I felt impressed again that we should try to rent empty apartments. I had mentioned this to a board member some time earlier.

At the time, he thought it was a terrible idea. "I own apartments myself. I would never let you put ten high school students in one of my apartments for a week. You couldn't pay me enough to make it worthwhile. I'd have to repaint the apartments after they left."

So I had abandoned the idea.

But now, as we finished praying, I felt impressed to explore this possibility again. I called the vice president of Lincoln Properties—the largest apartment owner in Dallas.

"Is there any way you would rent us your empty units?" I asked.

"We might be willing to help you, but on two conditions," he said firmly. "First, we want a guaranteed contract. Second, we want insurance on each apartment against damage of any kind."

"Thank you so much. We'll get to work." And I hung up.

Writing the contract was not difficult. Obtaining the insurance at a price we could afford was almost impossible.

Explo '72 was held at the height of the anti-Vietnam War movement in the United States. The FBI had informed us that a radical group was making plans to explode a bomb in our main meeting place—the Cotton Bowl. It had taken seven insurance companies to underwrite a fifty-million dollar liability and personal injury policy.

When we went back to these companies and asked them to insure five to ten thousand apartments, they were unwilling. So we talked with an expert in Chicago. He knew of only one company in America that might help us, and they happened to be headquartered in Dallas. He gave us the name of a man in the company we had to see. He doubted any one else would even be willing to discuss it.

Jerry Franks, one of our staff members, went to the company's office and asked for this man.

"He's never here at the office," the receptionist said. "He's always out on the road."

Then she looked up, surprised. "I don't believe it. There he is now, standing in the hall."

Jerry rushed to see him. "You're the person I have been told to see."

The man frowned. "I'm expecting a very important call. As soon as it comes, I'm leaving no matter what. But I'll talk to you until the call comes."

Jerry explained what we needed.

The man nodded, "I'm going to help you."

He led Jerry into the office of an underwriter. "Write this man an insurance policy for damage on apartments in the amount of $20,000 per apartment for as many apartments as he wants to cover. And charge him, oh, fifty cents a night per apartment."

The underwriter exclaimed, "We can't write a policy like that."

But this man said firmly. "I'm telling you to write this policy. Now write it."

Later, we found out why he had given us the insurance. This man had four daughters. The youngest, his pride and joy, had become a Christian six months earlier. During that time, she had been asking her dad if she could have a trip to Explo '72 as a high school graduation present.

That morning during her high school chemistry class, acid had accidently been thrown into her eyes. He was waiting for the call from the hospital to tell him whether his daughter would ever see again.

Did he help because he thought God might save his daughter's eyes? Were his daughter's eyes spared because he helped? I don't know.

I do know that with the insurance we got the apartments. I know that 30,000 high school students had housing. I know that during the week more than 20,000 people received Christ and 1,000 were called into full-time Christian service.

And I also know that I had nothing to do with it. God did it!

Had Bill Bright been able to solve my problems and find the cots, I would have missed one of the greatest lessons of my life.

As God's Word says, "He who calls you is faithful, who also will do it" (1 Thessalonians 5:24, NKJ).

Leighton
Ford

Beginning the
Real Race

Dr. Leighton Ford is president of Leighton Ford Ministries, which focuses on encouraging younger leaders to spread the message of Christ worldwide. He has spoken to millions of people in thirty-seven countries on every continent of the world.

Dr. Ford served as associate evangelist and later vice president of the Billy Graham Evangelistic Association. For many years, he was featured as the alternate speaker to Billy Graham on the Hour of Decision broadcast and had his own daily TV and radio spots in the United States, Canada and Australia.

Heralded by Time magazine as being "among the most influential preachers of an active gospel," Dr. Ford also *serves as chairman of the Lausanne Committee for World Evangelization.*

He and his wife, Jean, have become close friends to Vonette and me as we have served our Lord together in many different projects. I am sure you will be touched, as we were, by their warm witness to the faithfulness and sufficiency of our dear Lord as you read their story of the loss of their oldest son Sandy in 1981.

Time, they say, heals. Time also sets ambushes. On a cold, clear Carolina afternoon, driving by Myers Park High School, memories suddenly come flooding back.

I stop . . . park . . . walk around the track where he ran so many races. It has been nearly seven years since Sandy ran his last race, more than three years since he left us . . .

It had been a quiet, undistinguished day after weeks of hectic travel. Jeanie, my wife, and I were enjoying an evening at home together.

Shortly after nine o'clock, the phone rang. A woman's voice asked, "Is this the Ford residence?"

I identified myself. She continued.

"This is Dr. Brazeal from Memorial Hospital in Chapel Hill. Your son Sandy has had a heart problem. He's here at Memorial."

In the dead calm after the phone call, we were numb with disbelief. We were still dazed when Kevin, our youngest son, charged in from his Young Life meeting. We told him about Sandy. Then I called our daughter Deb; she burst into tears.

Jeanie and I talked briefly about driving up immediately or the possibility of me driving up alone. But there was no point in that. We would leave in the morning. I pulled the file on Sandy's first heart operation, laid away and forgotten for six years. The old nightmare was back.

The day after Thanksgiving, Sandy went in for surgery. The doctors told us it would be a difficult operation with only a slight possibility of death. He was rolled away about 7:15 A.M. We waited all morning and all afternoon. His surgery had lasted much longer than expected.

At 6:50 P.M. the door opened. A doctor I had never seen before came in. His face was solemn; so was his manner. He spoke quietly and deliberately. They had finished the surgery, and the problem had been corrected. But they could not get Sandy off the heart-lung machine. Suddenly, the terrible truth hit me: *His heart won't start!*

Everyone prepared for the worst: *Sandy has a problem; he may die.* We gathered and prayed. More quickly than I could believe, people began to arrive. We were whirling about in a maelstrom of calling, praying, crying and holding each other.

I went into the room next door and prayed, not for Sandy's healing this time, but just to pray. Suddenly, an upsurging sense of peace and strength came over me. Calmly, I went back to the others, and I touched Deb and Jeanie. The terrible anxiety that had built up all afternoon, though still there, was under control, for a time, as we continued to wait.

Sometime after 8 P.M. the door opened and the doctors came in. We read the worst in their faces before they spoke. "We never got him off the table."

Groping for control and understanding, Jeanie asked, "Has this ever happened before?"

"Yes, ma'am." The doctor offered no more; there was nothing more to say . . .

Just as I pass the starting line on the track, I wish Sandy could start his whole life again. But would we want him back if it meant going through all the pain and hurt?

Suppose God had come to us and said, "You can have Sandy. Here is what he is going to be like, but you can have him for only twenty-one years!" What would we have chosen? No question. We would take him again—and again.

Nobody could have told me three years ago how much we would miss him or for how long. There is nothing quite like the death of a child. I guess most folks think that in a few weeks or in a few months the pain is over. Maybe for some people. But not for me. Not for Jeanie.

I want so much to see him again. Watch his flying feet going around the track. See him duck his head in a moment of embarrassment. Watch him touch the corner between his eyes and his nose when he is thinking. See him pray, legs apart, long fingers pressing together—moving them up and down or pulling them apart when he can't get the right word. But the pain of death is its finality. Things are never the same again.

And yet they have gotten better. We can talk more freely about Sandy now. As a family we can laugh at his foibles, remembering how spacey he could be. But still I find it hard to look at his picture. Deb can't read his journals. Jeanie's eyelids began having spasms three months after he died. They are better but still not perfect. And still the questions come.

I walk around the final curve on the track past the green wall with the "Go Mustangs" sign, past the scoreboard. I stop and look down at the spot twenty yards from the finish line where his legs began to wobble in that final race.

Why? What happened that day? Why did his heart run away again? Why was his heart flawed in the first place? And why was he not healed?

71

"When a good man dies; what a waste, who can explain it?" That question headlined a newspaper story the Sunday after Sandy died. Many would say, "What a tragedy; his race was cut short." But that gives me pause. *Tragic* is a word from the ancient Greeks, not from the language of the Bible.

I have looked at a lot of Sandy's pictures since he died. And I have realized what a great difference it makes whether I look at them from the viewpoint of life or of death.

Here is what I mean. When Sandy was physically alive and with us, I would have looked at those pictures with more or less interest, regret or pride, with a sense of wonder at what he grew into.

Now, after his death, I look at each one with a little voice saying over my shoulder, "How tragic, that Sandy would live only until he was twenty-one."

It is the same way when I read his journal. A sense of tragedy keeps murmuring, "And he only had six months, or one month, or one week to live."

How important then to decide what is Sandy's true end! If twenty-one years *was* the end, then it does seem tragic.

But if eternity is his end, then I can look from his infancy to his manhood and see each part fitting into an eternal whole which is yet beyond my understanding, but not my hope.

In one view, death leads to the trash heap.

In the other, death is swallowed up in glory.

So as I think of the infant who became our grown-up son, I can imagine him a man who has become a glorious creature of eternity.

Philosophizing, however, does not take away the pain that twists my insides when I achingly miss him. But as

72

Jeanie has reminded me, "We have got to see things from Sandy's perspective."

Was twenty-one years enough time to make his life fruitful and meaningful? Or would it have taken seventy-three? Then why not seventy-four?

Isn't it what fills those years that matters? Is time just clock-time or opportunity-time—or God-time? Is it how long or how full? For Sandy, the cup of time was overflowing.

The year after Sandy died, Kevin and I were raking leaves and talking about how we missed him. Kevin said, "But, Dad, maybe Sandy's influence has been far greater than if he had lived. His life was like a very bright light—a spotlight—focused intensely. But his death has been a floodlight. It has covered a much wider area."

I have become convinced that John 12:23 is not just a metaphor but a literal truth. "Unless a grain of wheat falls into the ground and dies, it remains by itself alone; but if it dies, it bears much fruit" (NASB).

Life blossoming from death—that is God's way. It is the way of the cross. And we have seen how God has taken characteristics of Sandy, godly traits, and placed them into the friends who loved him. More compassion into one. More commitment into another.

Weeks after Sandy died, a letter came from the missionary under whose direction he worked one summer in France. He wrote:

> We are so earthbound. We assume that the main part of God's will and work is here on earth. I believe that not only the best is yet to come, but the highest will also be there . . . *God never wastes anything* . . . rather than being the end, this is the beginning!

So I stand here on the track. I want him. I want to see those pounding feet, the curly hair, the smile, the serious, thoughtful eyes. I want him to run not just here on the track, but all through his life.

With my toe, I draw a line where the finish line was, where Sandy finished his last race. But the finish line is also the starting line. And that is what makes the pain bearable. That is what undergirds the loss with hope. That is what makes the race worth running. Suppose that life is not the race. Suppose life is only the training season, and eternity is the real race.

Then Sandy's heart was beating, not just for a medley relay, not just for twenty-one years, but for eternity. The weight he carried—including a wounded heart—was preparing him for an eternal weight of glory.

Sometimes in my mind, I whisper, "What is it like, son?"

And I hear him say, "I can think so deeply, and every thought is clear. I can speak and express exactly what I mean. I can run and never get tired. I am so surefooted in the paths of glory."

So a son leaves a legacy for a father. I have determined to run my race for Christ to the end. And when that time comes, maybe our Savior will let him come running to meet me. Then with all the sons and daughters of the resurrection, our hearts will beat, and we will run for God forever.

Joe Foss

The Test of Time

The president of the National Rifle Association, Joe Foss has had many titles during his life. He is a retired brigadier general, a former governor of South Dakota, past football commissioner and television host. But what impresses me most about Joe is his zeal for Christ and determination to help anyone on a spiritual quest find the One who transformed his life.

On numerous occasions, Joe has faithfully encouraged others to surrender their lives to Christ following one of the most powerful testimonies I have ever heard.

Joe has a distinguished military career. He served in the Korean War as a colonel in the U.S. Air Force. A hero in World War II, Joe shot down twenty-six enemy planes. He is the recipient of the Congressional Medal of Honor and the Distinguished Flying Cross.

Joe relates several lessons he has learned, but his

greatest came after an experience that changed his life in the heart ward of a hospital.

There is only one way for me to relate the greatest lesson I've ever learned, and that is to mention some of the earlier lessons in my life that I thought were important.

Way back, I learned to stay within the guidelines my father set—or suffer the consequences. One such learning experience I remember well. I varied from my scheduled route in the drive to and from high school and had a slight accident. As a result, Dad made me walk a twelve-mile round trip to and from school for three months. That was my last variance while Dad was running the show.

When I went to college, the biggest lesson I learned was that studying was my responsibility. If I forgot to study the material, I flunked. I had to learn this fact the hard way.

Later, in the U.S. Marine Corps, I learned quickly that attention to duty was of number-one importance. In aerial combat my flight team and I had to work as a very close-knit unit. If we didn't, we were shot out of the sky by the enemy. The others and I were fortunate to become aces many times over.

Likewise, in politics I learned that you must be organized and have teamwork, or you lose the campaign. Learning this hard lesson the first time I ran for governor of South Dakota, I subsequently went on to win the gubernatorial elections for the next two terms.

And as commissioner of the American Football League, I soon learned that, in order for all the teams to operate strictly according to the constitution and by-laws, they had to be continually reminded. Some teams were always trying new ways to circumvent certain rules. This keeps the commissioner and his crew on the lookout for violations morning, noon and night.

As an actor and host in the television show business ("American Sportsman" and "Outdoorsman—Joe Foss"), I soon learned the importance of checking the words and statements that the writers wanted to put in my mouth. An unfortunate comment could cause stacks of angry, critical letters. Once I forgot to wear my glasses while fly fishing in a wind on the Big Hole River in Montana. Letters came in by the dozens letting me know I was setting a poor example because it was easy to lose an eye without them. In fact, a man who had previously worked for me wrote and indicated he had lost his right eye because he forgot his glasses while fly fishing.

The years rolled on, and I figured that I had learned all the lessons I needed. Then the day came when it looked as though I was about to die. While filming a show, I got arsenic in my system from chewing corn stalks that had been sprayed for corn bores. The arsenic, being a cumulative poison, went to my nerve centers and caused me to lose the use of my arms and sense of taste.

While I was in this condition, I became interested in the spiritual side of life. My wife Didi and several of her friends had been praying for me. At this time Didi got me to attend a small, Bible-teaching church. It was here for the first time that I heard the message of how to become a born-again Christian. The minister said that one must have a personal relationship with Jesus Christ and must receive Him as Savior and Lord. The minister spoke about Nicodemus coming to Jesus in John 3 and inquiring about being born again.

This was all Greek to me, for I had never studied the Bible. I only knew a little about God and Jesus, His Son. When the minister said, "I'm going to give those who don't know Jesus a chance to pray and receive Him," I was dumbfounded. He prayed, "Lord Jesus, I need You. Thank You for dying on the cross for my sins. I open the door of my life and ask You to come in and be my Savior and Lord. Thank You for forgiving my sins and giving me eternal life. Take control of the throne of my life and have me be the kind of person You want me to be."

As he prayed, I hesitated, thinking, *I can't do this.* Then it dawned on me: *Joe, you'd better get aboard now.* I prayed fast and caught up.

As time wore on, I still stayed in square one, but more people prayed for me. Some years later, I was flat on my back in a heart ward with pain in my chest. (It turned out to be pericarditis.) I came into the ward a bit nervous because I didn't know what was wrong. Five people were in there ahead of me. I noticed a TV set over each bed. I thought, *This will take up some of the time.* But as the nurse put me into the bunk, she explained to me that the show on that set would be my heart waves. This was Thursday night, so by Sunday I had been doing a lot of thinking. That Sunday morning I wished I could be in church. No one seemed to know or care that it was Sunday.

All of a sudden, the man next to me got a straight line on the heart monitor. The nurses and the doctor came running. They pulled the curtain and hooked him up to the "battery charger." In a matter of minutes, the loudest cussing I'd heard in a long time came from behind the curtain. Someone said, "He always does that."

That afternoon the curtain was pulled, and the man looked as though he wasn't long for this world. If only I knew enough, I could talk to him about Jesus. It was then, in answer to Didi's and others' prayers, that I made up my mind: *If I ever get out of here alive, I'm going to learn everything I can about the Lord and tell others about Him.*

Thanks to Didi, I did get highly involved in learning

how to tell others about Him and in speaking to groups through Campus Crusade for Christ. Learning how to tell others about Jesus Christ is the greatest lesson that I or anyone else can learn.

When folks ask me, "What, out of all the things you've done and all the honors you have received, do you rate as the highest?" I tell them, "When I asked Jesus Christ into my life as Savior and Lord. Nothing else compares with it." Coming to know Jesus Christ is the ultimate privilege of life. Without this one you are lost for all eternity. But my greatest lesson is learning how to tell others about Jesus.

Like a Tree Firmly Planted

How blessed is the man who
    does not walk in the
    counsel of the
    wicked,
Nor stand in the path of
    sinners,
Nor sit in the seat of
    scoffers!
But his delight is in the
    law of the LORD,
And in His law he meditates
    day and night.
And he will be like a tree
    firmly planted by
    streams of water,
Which yelds its fruit in its
    season,
And its leaf does not
    wither;
And in whatever he does,
    he prospers.
        (Psalm 1:1-3, NASB)

Daniel Fuller

Fitting Into God's Plan

Dr. Daniel Fuller has been a professor of hermeneutics at Fuller Theological Seminary in Pasadena, California, since 1953.

I first met Dan when we were students at Princeton Theological Seminary in 1946. The following year we transferred to Fuller Theological Seminary where we were both members of the first class. We became close friends, and I had the privilege of being best man in his wedding to his beloved Ruth. Dan was one of the first of a group of six to join the staff of Campus Crusade for Christ in 1952, and he led the ministry at the University of Southern California.

Dan tells of his longing as a young man to be an evangelist like his father and how the Lord led him into a

81

teaching ministry instead. His love for God's Word and his desire to introduce others to our Savior continue to be an inspiration to me after more than forty years.

At age thirty-seven, my father was a successful manager of a packing house for the orange growers around Placentia, California. But as he negotiated by telegraph with eastern buyers for the sale of his clients' fruit, he increasingly found himself asking, "Is this all there is to life—just trying to get two or three cents more for a box of oranges?"

Finally one day he went into a storage room in the packing house to talk to God about the possibility of becoming a minister. During his prayer, he felt called to resign from his prestigious position and to enroll in Bible classes under Dr. R. A. Torrey and the other godly professors at the Bible Institute of Los Angeles.

As I heard him recount this story in subsequent years, one particular idea stuck in my mind: The only thing worth doing in life is preaching the gospel. So when I awakened spiritually at age 14, I decided to be a pastor. Therefore, at the conclusion of college and World War II, I prepared for the ministry at the newly-founded Fuller Seminary.

By this time my father had about thirty years' experience—first as a pastor, then as a radio preacher with the "Old Fashioned Revival Hour," a program aired on more than 1,000 stations in America and on several short-wave stations overseas.

My father was talking of having me take over his broadcast when he could no longer continue. So while at seminary, I sought to gain experience by teaching a high-school Sunday school class and occasionally by preaching.

82

After I completed my studies, he gave me larger roles to play in his worldwide ministry. Then in May 1950, he asked me to take over the whole broadcast so he could have a Sunday off.

That day I performed passably in getting the audience in the Long Beach auditorium to stand and sing "Heavenly Sunshine" and in preaching the sermon. But during the last five minutes when I gave the "altar call," things went badly. My father, with his great gift of evangelism, always brought the broadcast to a triumphant climax by describing the many hands going up throughout the audience to the radio listeners. But at the end of my broadcast, I could report no decisions for Christ. Afterwards, I drove back to Pasadena in tears because I had failed before so many people.

In the years from 1950 to 1955, I took over the entire broadcast six more times, but *never once was I able to report even one conversion while on the air!* Graciously, however, decisions for Christ from my preaching were made right after we were off the air. Letters reporting conversions also came in.

Bill and Vonette Bright had been my close friends since seminary days—first at Princeton, then at Fuller. At my wedding in October 1950 Bill was my best man, and Vonette helped organize the ceremony. Soon after, he received a mighty vision from God to help reach the world for Christ starting with college students. God mightily blessed his new work at UCLA as he took gospel teams into sororities and fraternities, urging people to submit their lives to Christ.

The next fall I volunteered to do the same thing at USC, partly because I wanted to become an evangelist like Bill and my father. But as my team went from house to house along fraternity row having no results, I again felt frustrated and compared my ministry to that of Campus Crusade which continued to grow at UCLA and several other campuses.

Then during that fall of '52, the Lord taught me an important lesson. It began when the dean at Fuller Seminary phoned to say that a faculty member had just suffered a heart attack. He wanted me to take over the professor's class on an inductive study of the Gospel of Mark the very next day. I had learned the inductive method under Dr. Howard T. Kuist at Princeton in '46-47 and had written a master's thesis on the study of this book the preceding year at Fuller. The dean argued that I was the only person he could turn to in this emergency.

Rebellion welled up in my heart. I didn't want to divert energy away from evangelism at USC to teach at seminary. My experience in explaining inductive Bible study was even less than my experience in preaching.

Many of those first classes in Mark were failures. But as I continued to teach, surprising things started to happen. Students began to remark that they were being blessed. And at the banquet to honor the graduates given that next spring, two of them publicly singled out my class in Mark as particularly beneficial. The next day a faculty member complained, "How come you get such outspoken praise when the rest of us are lucky if we hear a faint echo of approval for our teaching?"

This confirmed the lesson that God had been trying to teach me since that first distressing broadcast in 1950. My failures on the radio and on fraternity row emphasized that He did not intend for me to be an evangelist. Rather, God's plan for me was to teach His Word.

So, except for years spent getting required degrees, I have taught at Fuller Seminary. But I still try to evangelize when an opportunity arises, for this is what Paul urged Timothy to do even though he might not have had that special gift (2 Timothy 4:5). Also, in teaching the Bible inductively all these years, I have let the biblical texts themselves

84

emphasize to students how they must make the furtherance of the gospel their first priority.

This method has borne fruit. Just a few weeks ago, for example, a couple who had ministered on the campus at UC Davis brought a young man to my class. "This is your great grandchild!" they proudly declared. One of my former students had influenced this couple, and this young man, in turn, was one of the fruits of their ministry—a third-generation follower of Jesus.

So the greatest lesson God has taught me is this: "(God) gives (gifts) to each one, just as he determines" (1 Corinthians 12:11, NIV). While fulfilling the Great Commission should always be our goal, we must leave it to the Lord to show each of us how we fit into His plan to make disciples of all nations.

Joe
Gibbs

There's Another
Side of Life

Few coaches have accomplished so much so quickly in the National Football League as Joe Gibbs, head coach of the Washington Redskins. Under Joe's leadership during the past decade, the Redskins have won two Super Bowls, played in three NFC Championships, won four division titles, and made six playoff appearances.

As I have come to know Joe personally, I have found that, in addition to being one of the great coaches of modern times, he is also a gifted, godly, dedicated man whose testimony for our Lord is a constant inspiration and challenge to me.

Joe is active in church and youth programs. He is the founder and chairman of the board of trustees of Youth For

JOE GIBBS

Tomorrow, a home for wayward teenage boys in Washington, D.C.

Recently he was the guest speaker at a Super Bowl Prayer Breakfast sponsored by Athletes in Action and attended by 1,300 guests. On this occasion, God used him mightily, as He does so many times, to touch the lives of all of us who heard him speak.

Joe relates how his experiences as a football coach taught him to live by God's standards, not the world's.

When I graduated from San Diego State College in 1963 as a physical education major, my goal was to be successful and happy. I looked around and decided that the world was advising me of three things.

First, if you want to be happy, you need to make money, gain position and power, and become president of a company. Or in my case, win football games.

Second, the world loves you and will be your friend. I felt I could lean on people as I embarked on the adventure of my life. Third, since you have only one life, please yourself and do your own thing.

So I began to make decisions about my life and where I was going. Soon I found that even though I made more money and won more football games, there was still an emptiness inside of me. So I tried harder to accomplish more, thinking that at some point I would be happy.

I spent sixteen years striving for success and happiness. Then in 1972, I took a coaching position in Fayetteville at the University of Arkansas. My wife Pat and I had just had our first child, so I started to make some serious decisions about my life and family. At the same time, I met a group of people who had a different philosophy and set of goals than I did and who had a personal relationship with the Lord Jesus Christ and a commitment to His cause.

You know what I discovered? What the world had been telling me wasn't true at all. There was another side to life—God's. His view was that the most important thing I would leave on this earth was not money, position, or even winning football games, but the relationship I had with Him and with others who love Him. And He began to teach me a different way of life.

First, I learned that money, position and power are not important compared to relationships. Let me illustrate.

In my second year at the Washington Redskins, we had the privilege of playing for the NFC championship against Dallas. We had just won a big game at home. I was really pumped up on myself.

I got up one morning thinking about how important I was. Pat reminded me, "Pick up your socks and your bathrobe." And she starting telling me about a problem one of our sons was struggling with.

I thought, *Why is she bothering me with this? After all, I'm an important guy on the verge of winning the NFC championship.* So I stormed out of the house, slammed the door and huffed off.

I usually pray in the car on my way to work. As I talked to God that morning, the truth of what I had done grabbed me. *When I leave this earth,* I thought, *it will not be the football games or the fact that I am head coach of the Washington Redskins that will count. All of that will wind up in an ashtray some day. But the influence I have on my wife and two children, on those with whom I've worked or helped, and the investments I've made in someone else's life will last forever.*

So when I got to work, I called home. "Pat, taking care

of our home is more important than what I am doing at work. I'm sorry for the way I acted."

Fame really is fleeting. Fifteen years from now, I'll be sitting on some corner someplace telling some older guy, "You know, I was the head coach of the Washington Redskins."

And this guy will probably turn to those around us and say, "This man is crazy. He thinks he was the head coach of the Washington Redskins."

And you know what I'll think about? How I wish I had spent more time with the ones I love than I did.

Secondly, I learned that the world lies when it says it is my friend.

We had a good football team in 1983. Our record was fourteen wins and two losses—and those two by only one point apiece. John Riggins, Joe Theismann and all our guys had played great. We were headed for the Super Bowl, and we were the favorites.

The Washington, D.C., newspapers were actually saying that I was a pretty sharp football coach. The worst part was that I was beginning to believe their words. I thought, *Hey, the world does really love me.*

But at the Super Bowl, everything went wrong for us. We were getting killed. We even had a punt blocked.

Suddenly, with only twelve seconds to go in the first half, we were on our own twenty yard line. I had to make a decision. Either we could fall on the football right there and come back in the second half, or we could go for the score.

On the sidelines, Joe Theismann was talking a thousand miles a minute. I said, "Shut up, Joe. We are going to take a chance. We have a couple of time outs left. We'll throw a screen pass and, if we happen to break out to midfield or something, call a time out. Then we will take a shot at the end zone, and maybe we'll get pass interference or something."

I figured that when a team is on the twenty yard line, eighty yards from the opposing goal, the defense does not play man-to-man coverage. It just doesn't happen that way. That's why I called this particular play. Sounded like a good idea, didn't it?

I called a screen pass to Joe Washington. Joe Theismann went back and threw to Washington. But one linebacker covered Washington man-to-man. The linebacker picked off the ball and ran twenty yards for a score that sealed our loss.

Suddenly, I went from being a sharp guy to being, as the *Washington Post* described it the next day, a "buffoon." That's the world's reaction. When you live by the world's standards, if you win the game, you're smart; but if you lose, you're booed.

But God loves us in good times and bad. He cares when we win the games, when we get the rewards. But He is even more real in our lives when we are having tough times. And He uses the hard experiences to change us and to give us a greater appreciation for our friends and family.

I have experienced the truth of God's love during many hard times. A few years back, for example, I decided I needed financial security. I wasn't satisfied to let God work in my life and to coach football. I wanted to make some business deals. Pat didn't want me to do it, but I didn't listen to the mate God had given me and made the investments anyway.

The next three years were probably the worst we have ever lived through. Finally, I had to get on my knees and admit to God, "I am bankrupt. We have lost everything we have. You are the only One who can straighten out this mess."

Over the next four years, I put the mess in God's hands. I went to all nine banks that were involved in my complicated financial deals and said, "Hey, I don't have this money, but if you are willing to help, I will work this out."

Miracle after miracle happened to untangle my financial problems. And God was with me through it all. Best of all, I discovered that He was more real to me during the tough times than the easy ones.

Third, I learned that the biggest lie the world tells us is that we have only one life to live, so we should do our own thing. But God's side is this: He has created us with a soul for one reason—to have a personal relationship with Him. When we try to fill our lives with anything other than Him, we will always feel a void inside no matter what we accomplish.

Maybe you have been in business for twenty, thirty or even forty years. You have been trying to accomplish something that will make you happy. But suddenly you stop and say, "What is the problem here? I am not happy."

I experience this as a football coach every day. If I live for the world's standards, I am not happy or successful. Only one thing fills my life with purpose: my personal relationship with God through Jesus Christ. That is a miracle.

God speaks supernaturally to us through His Word and changes our lives. He helps us influence others, and in the process, we find happiness and success. That, I have discovered, is the true reality.

Billy
Graham

An Example
of Humility

Billy Graham is a statesman among statesmen, a leader among leaders, who endeared himself to me forty years ago when he took a special interest in me and Campus Crusade for Christ when it was only a fledgling movement. In fact, the first one thousand dollars the ministry received was a gift from Billy.

In his worldwide ministry of more than forty years, Billy has preached the gospel in person to more people than anyone else in history. His love for the Lord, his integrity, and his genuine sense of humility have been a strong witness for Christ to the multitudes of the earth. Vonette and I are truly indebted to Billy and his wonderful wife Ruth for their friendship and encouragement through the years.

BILLY GRAHAM

A popular author, he has written fourteen bestselling books including Peace With God *and* How to Be Born Again.

One of Billy's greatest lessons came through the example of a godly man whom Billy met during one of his crusades. Here is his story.

It was January 1950; the place was Boston.

Our evangelistic meetings in Los Angeles the previous summer had drawn unexpectedly large crowds and unprecedented media attention. When we finished in L.A., we began planning for our next crusade to be held in Boston. But everyone warned us that Boston—sophisticated, cultured, and steeped in tradition—would be far different from any other city in which we had preached. Many, in fact, doubted that we should even attempt any meetings there.

But Dr. Harold John Ockenga, the dignified and scholarly pastor of Boston's prestigious Park Street Church, believed otherwise. Risking his personal reputation, Dr. Ockenga urged us to accept a ten-day series of meetings in his church.

At once it became clear that God was at work in Boston in an unusual way. Thousands had to be turned away from the initial meetings, and we frantically found ourselves scrambling to find larger venues. The city's five newspapers competed in giving the crusade front-page coverage, and the national media picked up the story. Day after day, hundreds turned to Christ through the crusade.

Surely, I thought, Dr. Ockenga must be taking great personal satisfaction and justifiable pride in what is happening and the important part he's played in bringing it about.

93

One day in the midst of the campaign, I stopped by to see him at the church. His secretary told me he was in his office and suggested I go on in. As I entered, however, I thought she must be mistaken, for Dr. Ockenga was not to be seen. Then a muffled sob caught my attention—and I discovered him prostrate on the floor, his head literally under the rug. He was praying as earnestly and fervently as anyone I have ever seen, humbly acknowledging his unworthiness and his total dependence on the Holy Spirit. He was beseeching God to pour out His blessings on the people of New England through the meetings. There was no hint of pride or self-satisfaction here.

For me, his example was a vivid and unforgettable illustration of one of the Bible's clearest commands: "Humble yourselves, therefore, under God's mighty hand, that he may lift you up in due time" (1 Peter 5:6, NIV). If Dr. Ockenga, with all his education and prestige and success, needed to humble himself before God, how much more did I!

God has taught me many valuable lessons throughout the years, but one of the greatest is that the Scriptures teach us we are to humble ourselves. Only then can He use us as He wills.

The Bible does not tell us to pray for humility, as if we should expect God suddenly to break through our pride and fill us with humble feelings. Instead, the Scripture teaches us to humble ourselves—to face pride and self-satisfaction honestly whenever they rear their heads—and then to repent of them and take whatever action is necessary to be humble before God. Time after time, when I have been tempted to take credit for something God has done, I have had to humble myself by turning to God and acknowledging my total dependence on Him.

Pride is deadly, and Satan will manipulate it every time to thwart God's work in us and through us—just as he did with Adam and Eve in the Garden of Eden. But God has said, "I am the Lord . . . I will not give my glory to another" (Isaiah 42:8, NIV). No matter how much God may use us, all the glory, praise and honor must go to Him and Him alone.

Jack
Hayford

The Miracle
of Aimee

Dr. Jack Hayford is the senior pastor of The Church On The Way of Van Nuys, California. What began as a temporary assignment to pastor eighteen people in 1969 has continued fruitfully, and today the congregation numbers more than 7,000 members.

Jack has long impressed and inspired me as a spiritual bridge-builder. He has a loving, gracious spirit that reaches out to embrace men and women of all denominations and movements that honor our Lord. He is a true ambassador of Christ's prayer, recorded in John 17, that His followers may be one even as He and the Father are one.

Jack is also a gifted composer, having written more

than four hundred songs, hymns, and other musical works, including the popular song "Majesty."

Jack has a special ministry teaching Christians how to worship and praise our wonderful Lord through song. Here he tells the heartwarming story of a little girl who taught him how personal and rewarding that worship can become.

She was the picture of shyness, standing at the door bashfully glancing my way, with one finger curled to her lower lip and her eyes eloquently inquiring, "Can I see you, Pastor Jack?"

I beckoned to her, and the eight-year-old walked across the prayer room to where I stood with some elders. I knelt to greet the child.

"Hi, Aimee," I smiled. "What do you want?"

She was so sweetly child-like. "Pastor Jack, I want you to hear a song the Lord gave to me."

Though the service was about to begin, right then she seemed a more precious and urgent matter than the multitude gathering for worship.

"Sing it for me."

She sang a tender little tune. The child's loving lyric voiced her worship and gave expression to her first discoveries in the Holy Spirit's creativity in song.

"That's beautiful, Aimee. You keep singing it to the Lord Jesus, will you?"

She nodded, and we hugged each other as I whispered, "Thank you for sharing your song with me. Tell Mama and Daddy hello for me, and . . . I love you."

Her smile would have melted a million hearts as she said, "I love you too." She slipped out the door and hurried to find her mom and dad.

There's more to Aimee's story, but for the moment I pause to underscore one of the greatest lessons I have ever learned about worship and song: *God wants to give everyone their own song of praise to Him.*

The Creator, whose Word repeatedly says, "Sing unto the Lord a new song," wants to beget a new song on the lips and from the hearts of His own—a distinctly new song of your own!

My response to Aimee's song was more than a pastor's kindness to a child; it was my confirmation of a vital practice. She had never heard me encourage private song-making in worship, but at her tender age she was experiencing a creative possibility open to us all.*

Worship may be possible without song, but nothing contributes more to its beauty, majesty, tenderness and intimacy. The breadth of style, the endless melodic possibilities, the delicate nuances of choral dynamics, the brilliant luster of instrumental arrangements, the soul-stirring anthems of anointed choirs, the rumbling magnificence of giant organs—all seem to be a God-given means for our endless expansion in worship.

What guidelines does God's Word offer us for expecting and cultivating music in corporate worship?

---

* Song-making and song-writing are two different things entirely. I do not even generally encourage people to think of the songs they sing spontaneously as songs to be written for others to sing. Of course, occasionally that will occur, but if the focus of worship-song becomes "song-writing," the pure simplicity of the practice becomes lost in one's preoccupation with memorability, the effect the song may have on others, the quality of the melody, the refinement of the lyric, etc. Song-writing for widespread use is a gift God gives to relatively few; song-making is a gift potential He has given to everyone.

First, the fruitful implanting of the Word of God is linked to our singing and worshipping (Colossians 3:15,16). Most of us consider these separate functions—the Word as instructional and song as inspirational. However, I believe worshipful song is needed for the meat of the Word to be assimilated into our character and conduct. Just as our digestive system is necessary to process food and distribute nutrients throughout the body, so worshipful singing is essential for the integration of the Word into our life.

Second, Holy Spirit-filled worship is the means by which God's precepts are infused into the human personality. Worshipful singing quickens our minds to receive the Word and submits our souls to the Holy Spirit's implanting it within us. Spirit-filled worship allows us to receive power through the teaching from the Bible.

There is no mystery to the message here: If you want to walk in God's will and wisdom, avoid the world-spirit and keep filled with God's Spirit—practicing song-filled worship is the way to do both!

One thing that did more to expand our own horizons in corporate worship came about through repeated frustration and failure: We couldn't get a choir to last.

Each new try involved capable people. Each beginning seemed exciting for everyone. But after three tries in as many years, I concluded God was trying to tell me something. I surrendered to the Lord the idea that we needed a choir. God's declared moratorium on our efforts to form a choir was the key to unleashing the song of our congregation.

I began to treat the church the way I would a choir. I didn't believe choirs were an unholy tradition that should be demolished, but rather that we were all to be "the choir" for the present season in our bodylife. (Incidentally, we still treat the body as a "choir," but we also have six vocal and two handbell choirs.)

99

The Book of Revelation unveils a massive angelic choir of worshippers in heaven: "And the number of them was ten thousand times ten thousand and thousands of thousands" (Revelation 5:11, KJV). But the Book of Hebrews goes further, and amazingly puts us *all* in that heavenly choir, there at God's Throne, sounding our praises beside the angelic choir, joining in the timeless worship of the Most High—*right now . . . every believer!*

> You have come to Mount Zion and to the city of the living God, the heavenly Jerusalem and to myriads of angels (Hebrews 12:22, NASB).

As these and other truths of God's Word began to register, something came unshackled! Suddenly the congregation perceived themselves in a new light—joined to the heavenly angel choir! Biblical truth had set them free to worship with a new sense of privilege and responsibility. Our absence of a formed choir became a pivotal point in releasing everyone to be "the choir."

Believers are learning to apply the power of song and worship to their everyday routine. It's not only contributing to the rise of homes filled with a holy happiness, but homes where the presence of God's Kingdom crowds out the efforts of hell to erode the peace and unity of families.

It doubtless seemed "just another Sunday" as Aimee's parents, Mike and Cheri, were seated with the congregation that day more than a decade ago.

Mike and Cheri were unable to have children. Medical examination had indicated that it was very unlikely they would ever enjoy that parental privilege short of adopting a baby.

Of course, I knew nothing of these facts nor of their prayerful desire that, after eleven years of marriage, they might conceive a child.

That Sunday my subject was "The Conceiving and

100

Bearing of Life." It wasn't really a message on having children, but on overcoming barrenness in the bleak spots of our life. Using "Sing O barren" from Isaiah 54 as my text, I discussed God's call to worship and to praise Him even when our lives seem hopelessly unfruitful. It was then that something very special took place. My understanding of at least one manifestation of the spiritual gift called "a word of knowledge" (1 Corinthians 12:8) is that the Holy Spirit will give someone *both* supernatural insight *and* a corresponding promise from God regarding the issue being revealed. While I was preaching, I paused, sensing the Holy Spirit's presence and prompting.

"Church," I said, "I need to interrupt myself for just a moment. The Holy Spirit is impressing me that there is a couple here this morning who long for a child and have been told they cannot have one. His word to you is this: 'Fill your house with song, and as you do, the life-giving power of song will establish a new atmosphere and make way for the conception you desire.'"

I didn't ask anyone to indicate their personal situation or response to that word. Rather, I simply went on with the message, basically forgetting the incident until nearly a year later when Mike and Cheri came up to me with a baby in their arms. Mike reminded me of what I had said about the couple who had longed for a child.

"Pastor, we went home that day to do what the Holy Spirit instructed us—we filled our house with song. Cheri and I walked hand in hand into each room and sang praises and worship to the Lord. We just wanted you to know that this baby is the fruit of that song, that the Lord did fulfill His word given that morning."

Can you imagine how I rejoiced with them?

That baby's birth was a holy phenomenon, not conjured up by man's efforts or enthusiasm. It was the precious fruit of one couple's natural union which, until the divinely appointed song of the Lord entered their situation, had not found the fruitfulness for which they longed.

I am especially touched as I remember the little eight-year-old girl who came to the prayer room door and sang "the song the Lord had given to her."

She was the fruit of a song—a song that now was finding a place in her young life.

Who knows what richness her song will bring as her years follow?

Who knows what a new song may bring to you?

Edward V. Hill

The Third World

More than twenty years ago, E.V. Hill spoke to about a thousand of our staff and students gathered at Arrowhead Springs for training. He boldly challenged us to come and witness for Christ in his Watts community, even though it was during the days of riots. He reminded us that his community had white insurance salesmen and white water meter readers, but no white Christians witnessing in black South Los Angeles.

More than a thousand of us went to live that weekend in the homes of the Christians of Mount Zion Missionary Baptist Church where E.V. has faithfully served as pastor for more than thirty years. Vonette and I stayed in the home of E.V. and his late wife Jane Edna. The weekend was an experience that had a dramatic impact on my own life as well as the lives of the staff and students who participated. More than a thousand blacks were introduced to Jesus Christ by our largely white staff and students.

Admired as one of today's great preachers and teachers of God's Word, E.V. is often asked to speak at conventions, conferences and revival meetings. He reaches a wide television and radio audience around the world. Multitudes have received Christ through his evangelistic efforts.

E.V. illuminates for us the effects of growing up as a black man in the United States and honestly relates his journey from anger, pain and hatred of white people to a love and compassion for them that is color blind.

There were two worlds in Guadalupe County, Texas: the white and the black. As children, we were encouraged to believe that if we went to school, remained in school and made good grades, someday we might be a part of the small percentage of Negroes who were acceptable Americans.

There was never a feeling of hostility on our part. As a community, we never blamed the white man. We said it was somehow his good luck that he had the upper hand.

Until I was twelve or thirteen years old, I had no particular problem with this way of thinking. I believed that it was just this way; we had two worlds—and there wasn't anything really wrong with this system.

White people said this separation was not due to just the fact that we were black, but to the fact that Negroes were at a lower point in their development. They said there wasn't a great deal of prejudice against the fact that we were black, but rather they objected to us because we weren't educated, carried many diseases, had a different blood type, weren't cultured, didn't have money, and weren't socially mature.

Therefore, most—including many Negroes—accepted this situation. Some of the black community accepted it because we were told that if we prepared ourselves, educated ourselves, became clean and free of disease and showed quality, then we would develop our own black society and, to some extent, become acceptable in the white community.

However, at about thirteen years of age, I learned, as did many Negroes throughout the United States, the hypocrisy of this "gospel."

We were always told that all whites were practically perfect. But we began to see that some whites were not clean, were not educated, and were filled with diseases. We learned there was nothing inherently different in our blood type as opposed to theirs.

We heard of Negroes who were educated, but who also received the same discrimination.

I was an active member of the 4-H Club at that time and raised livestock. I showed my stock in all of the Negro shows throughout the county, and I often won. I exhibited in major shows such as the Houston Livestock Show and the Dallas State Fair, but the limitations were always there.

For instance, Negroes could not show in the calf division; we could only show our hogs. We could only win the Grand Champion of the Negro section; our hogs were not judged against those of the whites.

I had an aspiration, a longing. I didn't hate, but I wanted to compete fairly.

I did not want to be white, but if I raised hogs better than the whites, why couldn't I receive the title?

Then suddenly I rebelled at the idea that there had to

be separate black and white worlds based on the premise that blacks were at a lower level—dirty, diseased and dumb. Clearly some of the whites were poor, uneducated, unclean, and much less earnest than many Negroes in their desire to excel; *we were thwarted because we were black.*

I could do nothing but hate such a system and hate the white people who were afraid to come out and compete fairly to earn their titles. We hated them for using the color of their skin as their only weapon of defense for the status quo.

This hatred boiled within me all through high school and on into college. It did not affect my relationship to the church, however. Somehow, I gained satisfaction from the Scriptures; for me, the white world and the white people who maintained that world were evil. Consequently, we just said, "The Lord will punish those evildoers."

I have often said that if the black militant movement had been alive in my era, it would not have been difficult for me to have led such a movement and to have called white people "blue-eyed devils."

Within my philosophy then, there existed no white Christian. The white church was established only to maintain white control. What about white people who had really experienced grace in their hearts and salvation through Jesus Christ? To me, there were none.

The real Christians were black people because they were like the Israelites who had been persecuted, held down, despised and rejected. Therefore, the white people could be nothing but the devil.

I knew no whites who were Christian enough, or who believed in Jesus enough, to take a stand against discrimination. They all said, "Obey the law, for this is the law even though it is wrong."

I became a confirmed black man who believed in

106

Jesus Christ, who knew of no whites who did, and who wanted nothing to do with them. The only connection I wanted with them was a chance, as a Negro, to become a greater man than they.

I hoped for a strong, materialistic, religious black race—not hostile to whites nor advocating the annihilation of them, but beating them, overcoming them, having more than they.

As a freshman at Prairie View College, the Negro auxiliary of the Texas A&M University system, I became involved in the Baptist Student Union and was selected to attend the National BSU Convention in Nashville, Tennessee. I had no money, but the BSUers at Texas A&M, through various projects, raised the money for two of us to attend. Both black and white students were going to this meeting.

I was happy to go, and I accepted the money the white students raised because I looked upon it as their attempt at pity toward a less fortunate person. I felt that they got a lot of glow and glee from knowing they sent a Negro somewhere.

Then my troubles began. This trip was to be by car, and in the car would be three whites and two Negroes. I was so filled with hatred and misgivings about the trip—traveling through the South—I almost backed out. However, I finally agreed to go. We met at Texas A&M in College Station and began the trip with a very distinguished gentleman, Dr. W. F. Howard, then director of student work for the Baptist General Convention of Texas.

There I was, totally disliking the whole set-up, but anxious to show the whites that I was their superior. I didn't know where we would eat or where we would sleep. Dr. Howard informed us that we would travel together, stay together, and eat together, and if there were places that

107

would not serve all, we would not eat at all. For the first time in my life, I had met a white man who acted like he was Christian enough to take a stand against injustice with a black, Christian brother. I couldn't believe it! I knew the moment would come when he would buckle under, but he never did.

Up to this point, I had known two worlds: the white world with its social, religious and economic systems and the black world with a separate church, economic and social system. For the first time, I began to understand that there was another world—a third world, a world of Christians. I discovered that within this Christian world there were both blacks and whites who had been regenerated to believe that the color of a man's skin really made no difference.

I also discovered that there were whites working constantly in their local churches to rid themselves and their communities of prejudice and discrimination. There was no beating of drums; they were not seen in the headlines—but they were working, and they were sincere.

I saw myself in the same condition in which I had seen the white community—filled with churchianity and justification of the flesh and empty of the Spirit of God. I too was a hypocrite.

It was on this trip and at this meeting that I invited Christ to have complete control of my life.

I am still an advocate of strengthening the Negro as a people—but not for the purpose of beating or ruling over someone. I now want to lead the Negro people to the many opportunities and the great fellowship of the third world— the Christian world.

I now look with prayerful compassion upon those white people who are fervent followers of Jesus Christ and who are sincerely witnessing and working daily to inform the white world that there is a Christian world.

I know the agony, the threats, and the danger they are experiencing daily. I, too, am in constant danger and under criticism and ridicule from those who feel that I am just another Negro who has gained acceptance in the white community and who is now simply saying to black people, "Be patient and quiet."

I now know that God did not create this world for the whites or the blacks, but He created it for Himself. But it is very difficult to explain to black people that there is a third world. I live in a community where many are almost at the point of denouncing Christianity. Some consider it synonymous with racism.

For the most part, the majority of my people are those who have experienced the joy, inspiration, emotion and fervor found in a Negro congregation of worship.

However, they have not yet experienced the reality of becoming a part of the third world because they have not received Jesus Christ. And so we labor daily, saying to men and women who are in the black world that there are many unfortunate and unjustifiable wrongs that have been committed toward us because we are black. There are many white churchgoers who use the Bible to protect their prejudice. But they do not truly represent Jesus Christ! They are not a part of His kingdom.

There is a third world where white and black men are planning, working and praying together, sacrificing and accepting abuse together, so that the kingdoms of this world will become the kingdom of our Lord (Revelation 11:15). "It is He who has made us, and not we ourselves" (Psalm 100:3, NASB).

Bill
Hybels

❦

Reading Your
Gauges

From 125 people in 1975 to an attendance of more than 14,000 today, Willow Creek Community Church, in South Berrington, Illinois, continues to be one of the country's fastest growing churches under the leadership of senior pastor Bill Hybels.

I was very impressed with Bill when he spoke at our International School of Theology graduation ceremonies some years ago. His message was profound and his love for our Lord was communicated through his scintillating personality. It was obvious that God had great plans for Bill, and I am deeply grateful for his insightful, powerful chapter in this book.

Bill is the author of a number of books, including Honest to God, Too Busy Not to Pray and a new release,

Fit to be Tied. *An internationally sought-after speaker, writer and consultant, Bill was also the chaplain of the Chicago Bears for five years.*

Despite a successful ministry and disciplined lifestyle, Bill found himself drained of emotional resources. He shares how he made an amazing discovery—that the mundane and ordinary things in his life provide a healthy balance to help him serve God for a lifetime.

For almost all of the eighteen years I have served in ministry, I have monitored myself closely in two areas, continually checking two gauges on the dashboard of my life.

Until recently, I thought that was enough.

First, I kept my eye on the spiritual gauge, asking myself, *How am I doing spiritually?* Apart from Christ I can do nothing. I know that. I don't want my life's efforts to be burned up because they were done merely through human effort, clever tactics or gimmickry. I am gripped by the fact that I must operate in the power of the Holy Spirit.

To keep my spiritual gauge where it needs to be, I have committed myself to the spiritual disciplines of journaling, fasting, solitude, sacrifice and study, among others. These clarify spiritual issues and pump a high-octane fuel which provides intensity and strength for ministry.

Second, I have monitored the physical gauge: *How am I doing physically?* If I push my body too hard, over time I will experience a physical breakdown or psychosomatic complications associated with high stress. If I don't exercise, eat properly and rest, I will offer the Lord only about two-thirds of the energy I have the potential of giving.

Since these spiritual and physical gauges—the only two on my dashboard—have consistently signaled "go," I have pushed myself as hard and fast as possible. But recently a different part of my engine began to misfire.

While preparing for a particularly difficult series of sermons, I couldn't seem to get the message to come together. No matter how hard I tried, no ideas seemed worth saying. Suddenly I found myself sobbing with my head on my desk.

Individuals more aware of their feelings might have known what was wrong, but I didn't. So when I stopped crying, I said to myself, *I don't think that was natural.*

I forced my thoughts back to the sermon and managed to put something together for the service.

But the next morning as I wrote in my journal, I thought, *Am I falling apart in some area spiritually?* My gauges said no. *Physically, am I weak or tired?* No, I felt fit.

I concluded that maybe this was my midlife crisis, a phase I would simply have to endure. But four or five similar incidents in the next few weeks continued signaling that my anxiety and frustration could not be ignored.

After a Christmas vacation that didn't change my feelings, I began to seriously inspect my life. I talked with several respected people and learned that I had overlooked an important gauge: emotional strength. I needed a third gauge on the dashboard.

I slowly began to realize that certain activities drain my emotional reservoir. Because I am a minister, I now call these experiences IMA's—Intensive Ministry Activities.

An IMA may be a confrontation, an intense counseling session, an exhausting teaching session, or a board meeting about significant financial decisions. Preparing and delivering a message on a sensitive topic which requires extensive research and thought also wears me down.

The common denominator of these activities is that they sap you, even if only for a few hours. Not realizing this, I was oblivious to the intense drain I was experiencing.

Something was wrong. I needed that third gauge—an emotional monitor—to determine my ministry fitness.

I have now committed myself to installing an emotional gauge in the center of my dashboard and learning how to read it. Now I monitor my emotional resources so I don't reach that point of fatigue. What signals do I look for?

If I drive away from a ministry activity and say, "It would be fine if I never did that again," that's a warning signal. Something is wrong when I look at people as interruptions or see ministry as a chore.

Another indicator: On the way home, do I consciously hope Lynne isn't having a problem and my kids don't want anything from me? That's a sign I don't have enough left to give. When I hope that the precious people in my life can exist without me, that's a sign of real trouble.

A third check for me is how I approach the spiritual disciplines. I journal and write my prayers. For months I found myself saying, day after day, "I don't have the energy to do this." I journaled anyway, but more mechanically than authentically. I dislike myself when my Christianity is on autopilot.

Each person has to find the warning signals for his or her own life. But after an IMA, it helps to ask some questions of yourself: *Am I out of gas emotionally? Can I not stand the thought of relating to people right now? Do I feel the urge to take a long walk with no destination in mind? Am I feeling the need to go home, put on music, and let the Lord recharge my emotional batteries?*

My next discovery was humiliating. I found that when my emotional fuel was low, I couldn't do an Indy pit stop and get a fast refill. Replenishing emotional strength takes time—usually more time than it took to drain.

The best analogy I can offer is a car battery. If you sit in a parking lot and run all your car's accessories—radio, headlights, heater, horn, rear window defogger, power windows—you can probably sap that battery in about ten minutes. Suppose you then take the battery to a service station and say, "I'd like this battery charged. I'll be back to pick it up in ten minutes."

What would they tell you? "No, we're going to put the battery on our overnight charger. It's going to take seven or eight hours to bring it all the way back up." It has to be recharged slowly or else the battery will be damaged.

Likewise, to properly recuperate from an emotionally draining activity takes time. When I see my emotional gauge is reading low, I take time to recharge. Some people recharge by running, others by taking a bath, others by reading, others by listening to music. Usually it means doing something totally unrelated to ministry. The important thing is to build a ministry schedule that allows adequate time for emotional recharging.

I've learned a second thing about maintaining emotional resources for ministry. The use of your major spiritual gift breathes life back into you. When you have identified your spiritual gifts and use them under the direction of Jesus Christ, you feel the affirmation of God, and many times you feel more energized *after* than before.

Conversely, serving outside your gift area tends to drain you. If I were asked to sing or assist with accounting, it would be a long hike uphill. I wouldn't feel the affirmation of the Spirit because I wouldn't be serving as I have been gifted and called to serve. This is why many people bail out of various types of Christian service: They aren't in the right yoke.

Unwittingly I had allowed myself to be pulled away from using my strongest gifts. My top gift was leadership. My second gift was evangelism. Down the list was teaching and administration.

In order to adequately prepare my messages, I had slowly delegated away almost all leadership responsibilities. And too often, in elder or staff meetings, I was mentally preoccupied with my next message. My life became consumed by the use of my teaching gift, which wasn't my most fruitful or fulfilling ministry. Yet people kept saying, "Great message, Bill." And I wrongfully allowed their affirmation to thwart my better judgment.

Since realizing this, we have implemented a team-teaching approach at Willow Creek. It has been well received by the congregation and has allowed me to provide stronger leadership in several areas. It would be difficult for me to describe how much more fulfilled I'm feeling these days.

I have also found new opportunities for evangelism. Recently I met with three guys at an airport. One was a Christian, and the other two were his best friends whom he was trying to lead to Christ. As we talked, I could feel the Holy Spirit at work. After our conversation ended, I ran to my gate, and I almost started crying.

I love doing this, I thought. *This is such a big part of who I am. I used to lead people to Christ, but I've been preparing so many messages in the past five years that I've forgotten how thrilling it is to share Christ informally with lost people.*

God knew what He was doing when He distributed gifts for service. As we minister in a way that is consistent with the way God made us, we will find new passion for ministry.

Finally, becoming emotionally depleted re-taught me a lesson I had forgotten—that a Christian leader has to strike a delicate balance between involvement in the eternal and

115

involvement in the mundane. The daily things of life provide needed counterweight to timeless truths.

When we started the church in 1975, I had discretionary time that I used to race motorcycles, fly a plane, golf and ski. I had relationships outside the congregation and interests other than the church.

Since that time, the needs of the church inexorably squeezed out these earthly pursuits. I became consumed with the eternal. I'm an early riser, so from 5:30 in the morning until I crash at 10:30 at night, barely one moment of time is not related to something eternal. I don't exercise at the YMCA anymore; I work out on equipment in my basement. While I'm cycling, I read theological journals. When I pump weights, I listen to tapes or think of illustrations for a message. The eternal co-opted the daily routines.

Spiritually, I was fine—I had maintained my disciplines and was striving to obey Christ. Physically, I held up fine—it wasn't like running a marathon. But I was totally depleted emotionally.

I was filling my life chock full of eternal opportunities.

What's wrong with that? Besides the emotional drain, I realized two other hidden costs of such a ministry-centered lifestyle.

First, if you are concerned only with spiritual activities, you tend to lose sight of the hopelessness of people apart from Christ. You're never in the world.

Second, you lose your wonder of the church, of salvation, and of being part of the work of God. You can overload on eternal tasks to the point that you no longer appreciate their glories. Having enough of the mundane in my life makes me see the futility of the world and the wonder and delights of the Christian life.

I'm convinced God wants me to live in order to finish

the race I've started. Knowing this, my goal is to monitor my spiritual, physical, and emotional resources so that I can minister, by God's grace, for a lifetime. That's the challenge of every Christian leader. And monitoring all three gauges— spiritual, physical and emotional—plays an important part in our longevity.

Marvin
Kehler

How My
Commitment and
Conviction Grew

When Marvin Kehler came to a Campus Crusade for Christ seminar held at our international headquarters, he was a successful young businessman in British Columbia. During his stay, God began to give him a vision for investing his life in helping to fulfill the Great Commission. Four years later, he became the director of Campus Crusade for Christ in Canada, a position he holds today.

Marvin began his business career by taking over his father's egg producing operation. Within a few years, it was the third largest in British Columbia. He expanded into many other businesses including contracting, industrial, electrical, mining and land development.

Through Marvin's creative genius and dedicated life, he and his wife, Kathy, who leads the National Prayer Ministry for Canada, have touched the entire country for the glory of God. And he holds a deep vision for reaching men and women for Christ. His story tells how he first learned to share God's love and forgiveness with others and how this changed his life.

My wife, Kathy, and I have always wanted to live meaningful, dynamic lives—not just to maintain the status quo. Together we worked hard to be successful in our egg producing and wholesale operation while raising four active children. I was also president of the British Egg Producers Association and a construction company.

Our lives were packed with activity. We were motivated by material pursuits, but we also served in our church. I was an elder and the youth director; Kathy led the Sunday school choir and helped begin a Pioneer Girls club.

We also enjoyed family hobbies: snow skiing in the winter, water skiing and competing at various west coast horse shows during the summer.

We loved the fast-paced, active lifestyle. But after a while, the challenge and novelty wore thin. I began to ask some serious questions. Where was I heading? I was supposedly happy, yet why did I feel so empty inside? Why did my successes seem so futile and meaningless?

Then someone encouraged us to attend a five-day seminar at the International Headquarters of Campus

Crusade for Christ. What we heard there changed our lives! We learned how to yield to God on a moment-by-moment basis and to be controlled and empowered by His Holy Spirit. And God showed me through His Word that my self-reliance was keeping me from experiencing His supernatural power at work within me.

As part of the training, we were shown how to share our faith in the community. When I stood ready to press the first doorbell, I said to God, "You have to help me. I have nothing to say."

Suddenly, a voice inside me said, "Marvin, I am glad you realize that. I will give you the words to say."

That afternoon, for the first time in my life, I led someone to Jesus Christ. It was exciting to see God use me in this way.

Later that week, Dr. Bright challenged the conferees to "Come help change the world." Together, Kathy and I committed ourselves to go wherever God wanted us to go, do whatever He wanted us to do, say whatever He wanted us to say and give whatever He wanted us to give.

When we returned to Canada, we re-evaluated all our priorities in light of helping to fulfill the Great Commission. Our conviction and commitment grew. We now shared our faith in a more effective way with our youth group and neighbors and soon experienced a spiritual awakening in our community.

What we were doing began to be multiplied into many people's lives. Many were carrying on with evangelism and discipleship—some full-time, others part-time. For example, Jack and Carol Klemke, an Alberta businessman and his wife, attended one of the seminars in Canada. They, too, accepted the challenge of helping to fulfill the Great Commission in this generation. Over the years, they have trained thousands of lay people in western Canada and hosted many, many evangelistic dinners for business and professional people. Later they were used by God to begin the Christian Embassy in Ottawa. Many members of Parliament and foreign diplomats have heard the message of God's love and forgiveness because of the Klemke family's availability and generosity.

Jack and Carol have also sponsored delegations of members of Parliament and businessmen to give their testimonies before presidents, heads of state, and political and business leaders in fourteen countries in Central America, Africa, and Europe, including the USSR and Poland.

Today, in leading the Canadian Campus Crusade for Christ ministry and in helping guide the Western European Crusade ministry, God has given me the privilege of working with a tremendous team of like-minded people. We have the satisfaction of sending between 200 and 650 people each year on "JESUS" film projects and Christian Embassy tours. God has also enabled our ministry to contribute millions of dollars to help fulfill the Great Commission in more than sixty countries. I can't help but thank the Lord for His faithfulness in allowing me the privilege to be a part of this great worldwide spiritual harvest.

D. James
Kennedy

———◆◆◆———

Shedding My Broad
Yellow Stripe

Dr. D. James Kennedy is the senior minister of Coral Ridge Presbyterian Church in Fort Lauderdale, Florida, and founder and president of Evangelism Explosion International, which teaches laymen in 105 nations how to share their faith in Christ. His weekly messages are televised to 33,000 cities and towns in America and fifty-seven other nations and territories.

Jim has long been a favorite of mine since I met him when he was a young pastor many years ago. At that time his church was located in a building with folding chairs next to a fire station, but he and different members of the congregation demonstrated even then a great burden for introducing others to Christ. I have followed his great progress with prayerful interest and am always blessed when I hear him speak in person or on television.

Jim is the author of more than a dozen books and in 1984 was selected as Clergyman of the Year by Religious Heritage of America. He served as moderator of the General Assembly of the Presbyterian Church in America in 1988-1989.

You will enjoy his account of how he learned to tell others about Christ. His insights into the importance and necessity of training in evangelism are presented through humorous encounters with "the Hulk."

Whenever I heard of a minister who was noted for evangelism, I formed a stereotype of what he was like: a bold extrovert who grabbed people by the lapels and shouted, "Brother, are you saved?" That is about as foreign a description of myself as I can possibly imagine.

In fact, I have always considered myself shy, particularly when I tried to witness. Talking to others about Christ was extremely difficult for me. I could hardly say "Good morning" to a complete stranger, much less bring up something as personal as religion.

But I sensed God's call into the ministry and went to seminary, graduated, and came to Fort Lauderdale to start a new church. I was full of vim and vinegar, a veritable Daniel come to judgment. I preached everything I had in every sermon. That wasn't a whole lot, but nevertheless I gave it what I could.

My team and I gathered about forty-five heterogeneous pagans into an un-air-conditioned cafetorium at 8:30 on Sunday morning. And I preached the greatest sermons in the history of the church . . . by Spurgeon and MacLaren and Luther and Calvin.

So powerful was my preaching that in ten months I had taken that struggling band of forty-five people and built it into a mighty army of seventeen. Any way I looked at it, I had about two and a half months of ministry left until I would be preaching only to my wife, who was threatening to go to the Baptist church down the street.

So I decided to try something different. If the mountain wouldn't come to Muhammad, then Muhammad would go to the mountain. I would visit somebody and would proclaim the gospel to him right where he was.

I had a valid reason why I didn't usually do that sort of thing. You see, I have always suffered from a serious back ailment. This broad yellow stripe goes right down my back and somehow or another connects to my jawbone which renders me absolutely silent in many circumstances when the less circumspect would have opened his mouth.

In spite of the back defect, I decided to visit anyway. I picked a visitor's card with shaky handwriting that looked like it had been signed by a little old lady. If I couldn't out-talk her, I could at least outrun her, even with my back problem.

So a layman and I knocked on the door of this home and waited for the little old lady with grey hair to open it. Instead, we found ourselves staring at the belly button of someone vastly different and very big—the Hulk. He wore an undershirt, held a can of beer, and clenched a cigar in his mouth. He was just my sort of person—the type I had been looking for to begin my witnessing career.

So I said to him, "Is Mrs. Jones home?"

"Nah."

"Thank you very much," I muttered politely and started to leave.

"Whatya want with her?" he demanded.

"Nothing. Nothing at all. Ah, the fact of the matter is, I'm the pastor of this little church down the street. Your mother visited us last Sunday, and I was just returning the compliment. Just tell her we dropped by."

Then this guy said one of the nastiest things I have ever heard come out of the mouth of any human being in a situation like this. Right out of the blue he said, "Come in."

Can you believe that?

I walked into that living room with my knees knocking. We sat and had an enlightening and edifying conversation about the weather. We progressed to sports. He was a Golden Glove fighter. I got off that subject in a hurry and moved to the news. Then back to the weather. It was getting warm.

The layman with me said, "Sic him!"

"Hush, man." I whispered. "You'll get us both killed. I'm working up to it."

Fact is, I had been working up to it for years. I just wasn't up to it any way you looked at it.

Finally, with great chagrin, I told this man (God forgive me) how much I had enjoyed the visit. We excused ourselves and left. And you know, I couldn't even look at my layman friend all the way back. Not only would the mountain not come to Muhammad, but Muhammad couldn't even climb a molehill. It was a very embarrassing situation.

When I got back home, I prayed earnestly, "Lord, what am I doing here? Surely this is all a big mistake. You didn't call me into the ministry to miserably fail." I wondered if I should leave the ministry and take up something else.

About that time, I got a letter from a preacher in Atlanta who wanted me, believe or not, to conduct ten days of evangelistic services. That's right. Me. The one who had almost decimated one church. Now he wanted me to ship it across state lines. "Have plague, will travel."

I picked out some of "our" sermons and headed north, happy to get away from my Lauderdale fiasco. When I showed up, I told this fellow, "Well, here I am. I'm ready."

He said, "That's great! You'll be preaching every night."

"Wonderful."

"However, that's not the most important thing."

Suddenly a cold chill went right down my yellow stripe. I thought, *Oh, Lord, don't let this guy say what I think he's going to say next. He looks like "that type."*

Sure enough he was. He announced, "Every morning and afternoon, we are going to go out into the homes and sometimes at night after the services. You're going to have an opportunity to witness to these people eyeball to eyeball, toenail to toenail. I've saved all the tough nuts for you."

Thanks a lot, I thought.

"That's great," I said confidently. "Actually, we professional evangelists don't like to fool with anything but tough nuts. To be perfectly honest, in my whole ministry, I've never dealt with anything but tough nuts. There's just one problem, however. I came to Atlanta to tell you that I wasn't going to be able to come because of this funeral you are going to have in town if I don't get out quick."

No, I didn't say that. I was trapped, and I didn't know what to do. I went back to my hotel room that night and got down on my knees and prayed, "Oh, Lord, what am I going to do now? I don't know how to witness to anybody."

You know what happened? Nothing. So I got down on my face on the floor and prayed for hours. "Lord, you've got to help me! I can't do this. I am absolutely desperate. This fellow is coming to get me in the morning. You've got to do something!!"

The most amazing thing happened. Morning came. The preacher picked me up. We went to a home and knocked on the door.

The door opened. Remember that big hulk of a fellow in Fort Lauderdale? He had moved to Atlanta. Well, not really. It was his bigger cousin, I think. As we went in, my mind quickly went over the latest news, sports and weather. Then this preacher blew the whole morning.

"Well, Hank," he said proudly, "I brought this professional evangelist out here to talk to you about your soul." And he pointed to me!

I gulped hard a couple of times and glanced at the preacher, then at the Hulk. I looked up to the Lord, trying desperately to grasp for something. All of a sudden I remembered a text, "Do the thing you fear." (I think that's 2 Ecclesiastes 3:2.) So I jumped right in, feet first.

In no more than twenty minutes I had that big fella ... furious. He was getting redder, and I was getting whiter by the minute. Suddenly, a flash of illumination came right out of Systematic Theology 302B. The man was evidently "non-elect." I felt better immediately.

Meanwhile, my pastor friend had come to a very different conclusion—that I was a "non-evangelist." In fifteen minutes, he had this man on his knees accepting Christ. That was very traumatic for a budding theolog. The "non-elect" got converted right before my eyes.

During those ten days of meetings, fifty-four people came forward. On any given evening, I could have told you who would respond because I had seen the pastor lead them to Christ during that week.

That was an amazing experience to me. I said to the pastor, "This is absolutely incredible. I saw a murderer accept Christ. I saw an adulteress accept Christ. And all sorts of people in between. How in the world did you ever learn to do this?"

"It was in this very same evangelistic crusade last year," he told me. "We really had an evangelist. He took me out with him, and I learned from watching him. A year ago, I didn't know how."

Well, I learned from watching this fellow. But there was one question buzzing around my mind as I was flying home: *This works in Atlanta, the heart of the Bible belt, but will it work in Fort Lauderdale?*

I found out that it does; it works anywhere that it's tried—in the inner city and the outlying rural regions. It works in America and Canada and England and Africa and Hong Kong and Singapore and Australia. It works because "it" is nothing other than believers carrying the gospel of Jesus Christ to others, just as He said we should.

I started witnessing to people everywhere, and people responded. After about a year, I stopped and panted breathlessly, "You know, there's only a certain number of people I can reach." Then I had an idea! Why don't I teach others to do the same thing? That's where Evangelism Explosion really began.

I took an elderly man who had been a Christian about sixty years with me. He had always wanted to lead someone to the Lord and never knew how. He went with me for months and months; I thought I would never get rid of him. Finally I put both feet in the small of his back and pushed him out of the nest. And he began to lead a lot of people to Christ.

Then there was another man I took out for a month or so. He went on vacation and called me the next week. He had led somebody to Christ. I prayed, "Lord, this is it. This is the way."

It wasn't until somebody took my hand and led me out that I began to overcome the blinding fear that silences so many people in the church. This is what Jesus did. He called the disciples that they should be "with Him."

Dear friends, the greatest privilege and responsibility you will ever know is to lead another person to Jesus Christ. And to equip the saints to do the work of ministry as Christ instructed us. You will find, as I did, that that is the greatest lesson you could ever learn.

C. Everett Koop

God's Sovereignty Remains My Greatest Comfort

A pediatric surgeon with an international reputation, Dr. C. Everett Koop served as Surgeon General of the United States from 1981 to 1989. Today he continues to educate the public about health issues through the C. Everett Koop Institute of Health and Science and as chairman of the National Safe Kids Campaign.

Dr. Koop's reputation as a brilliant surgeon and dedicated Christian came to my attention long before he became Surgeon General. His love for Christ and his faithful, courageous witness for Him have been an inspiration to me since we met many years ago.

C. EVERETT KOOP

In his account, Dr. Koop relates the lesson he learned through the death of his son. His story will give you a sense of security in knowing God's perfect plan for your life.

As I enter my seventy-fifth year, it seems I have learned many lessons; to label one of them the greatest causes me to look back at many situations, events and dilemmas.

I can say without hesitation that my greatest lesson has been learning that I have a sovereign God. He has taken me through many trials, which I certainly wouldn't have chosen for myself. He has taught me again and again that He has a plan for my life, and He will take me through the roughest and most painful of times with the tenderness and support that only a heavenly Father can give his earthly child.

The most clearly etched lesson that I learned about having a sovereign God who makes no mistakes occurred some years ago when our wonderful twenty-year-old son, David, was taken from us in a sudden, totally unexpected incident.

David was a junior at Dartmouth College in New Hampshire. He was climbing the granite face of Cannon Mountain, just above the Old Man of the Mountain in Franconia Notch. A large slab he was scaling loosened and carried him off the face of the cliff with it. David was roped to a companion, and when he came to the end of his tether, he was many feet below. Jerked to a halt, he then fell inward like a swinging pendulum, smashing his body into the face of the cliff. His companion lowered him to a narrow ledge, quickly secured the rope, then rappelled down to him. David had disrupted his right knee and bled to death on that ledge

131

despite valiant efforts on the part of his companion to revive him with artificial respiration. It was an injury that anyone could have kept from proving fatal had it occurred on the ground and a tourniquet been applied.

Word of David's fall reached the college hours later. And then on that memorable Sunday evening, the dean called me at home to relay the unbelievable news that David was dead. Our grief was bone crushing.

We were fortunate to have two of our children living at home and the remaining son and his wife only a mile away. We didn't know where or how to begin to cope, so I drew my family close and prayed a prayer that only the Holy Spirit could have inspired, asking God to be very close and give us the support we so desperately needed. I thanked Him for taking David to be with Him and then closed by asking Him to let us see blessing come from a tragedy that hurt us beyond description.

I don't know what we expected of that prayer—I certainly know it didn't come naturally from a heartbroken father—but we all sensed a peace from knowing a sovereign God was in charge.

When a child is taken, the reality of one's faith either sustains and comforts or, if not rooted in a loving God, falls apart. In the weeks and months and even years that followed, we saw God's hand at work in the aftermath of our loss.

Just the absence of bitterness in our children was remarkable. They developed a greater closeness to the remaining family which continues to this day. And each child was locked onto his or her own faith in a loving, sovereign God. What greater blessing could we ask?

One of the greatest spin-offs was our ability to put behind us the "what ifs" and "if onlys" concerning David's accident—the common quagmire which can hold parents and siblings in the continuing inability to recover.

132

C. EVERETT KOOP

As a pediatric surgeon, I gained a new depth of empathy and understanding when I had to deal with the parents of dying children. They knew I meant it when I said, "I know what you're going through."

Learning a lesson usually implies going through a difficult process—with emotions varying from mild anxiety to devastation depending upon the experience. It is certainly true that we grow and mature spiritually through adversity—not when everything is going smoothly. This, in a sense, is true for Christian and non-Christian alike. But in a time of adversity or trouble, the Christian has the opportunity to know God in a special and personal way. Indeed, it necessitates acknowledging our own inability to cope. It is then that we learn we must rely completely on the grace and mercy of a loving God. And how wonderful to know we have a Lord who knows the end from the beginning! A God who has fashioned our lives according to His perfect will! We sometimes seem to forget that important fact.

God's sovereignty remains my greatest comfort in all things, but the outworking of His perfect plan for me and my family at the time of David's death—our greatest distress— was surely my greatest lesson.

133

Tim LaHaye

❦

The Decision That Saved My Life

Tim LaHaye is an author, minister, television and radio commentator, and family life speaker. As founder and president of Family Life Ministries, Tim is being used of God to strengthen families throughout the United States and Canada by teaching them biblical principles.

Tim and his wife Beverly, who founded Concerned Women of America, are being uniquely used of God as few other people to help awaken the Christians of America to our God-given responsibilities in government, media and education.

At present Tim produces Capital Report, a Christian radio commentary on news events affecting the family, traditional moral values and religious liberty. He is the author of many books, including The Act of Marriage *and* Spirit-Controlled Temperament.

Here Tim describes his struggle to control a bad temper. The result will thrill you and give you hope for facing your worst habits in the power of the Holy Spirit.

Listening to Dr. Henry Brandt present his last message at a Gospel Light Sunday School Conference at beautiful Forest Home Christian Camp was a highly combustible Choleric/Sanguine minister. Typical of his temperament, he was a workaholic, pastoring a dynamically growing church which was one month away from dedicating a new church auditorium. He didn't have ulcers—he was just spitting blood!

Brandt hadn't been speaking more than four minutes when the young pastor became blazing mad. He assumed his wife had invited him to come to the conference so that the Christian psychologist could preach to him, "Do not grieve the Holy Spirit of God . . . Let all bitterness, wrath, anger . . . and evil speaking, be put away from you . . . And be kind to one another, tenderhearted, forgiving one another, just as God in Christ also forgave you" (Ephesians 4:30-32, NKJ).

Dr. Brandt told the unforgettable story of another young minister in the midst of a building program who was bleeding inside with ulcers. Three specialists told the bleeding minister, "We cannot find one thing wrong with you—you need an analyst." Being a Bible-believing minister, he didn't want to go to a secular "shrink," so he called Dr. Brandt, "a Christian psychologist" whose office was five hundred miles away, and made three appointments. When Dr. Brandt asked him who he was mad at, he blew up because

Dr. Brandt had suggested he was angry. The listening pastor got the message. He was just a few weeks behind the ulcerated minister of the story.

For the first time, this dedicated, hard working, Bible-teaching pastor realized something about himself. He was not a godly man! He had tried to be. He loved God; he loved to serve Him and had led many to Christ and the church. He worked hard at maintaining a morally pure mind. But now for the first time, he realized he was a sinful pastor—he often grieved the Holy Spirit with his temper.

His anger had affected his marriage. Only a loving, godly wife could have put up with him during those years—and that at great sacrifice. The entire family was afraid of him.

But now for the first time, he saw his sin and how he had limited God's use of his life. And that is the first giant step toward victory over anger—face it as sin. Don't justify it; confess it! When Dr. Brandt finished his message, the young pastor, under deep personal conviction over his angry spirit, went out to the prayer chapel to pray. Finding it occupied, he lay face down under a pine tree and poured out his heart to God.

This was the first time he was consciously filled with the Holy Spirit. Guess how God characterized Himself to this man? Peace! Incredible Peace! At last the war within was over.

How long do you think it lasted? Two and a half hours! Just until the mindless driver of a red sports car cut him off on the freeway and almost caused him to wreck his car. Instantly, he blazed with anger. Then he recognized he had lost the peace, so he confessed his sin again and was restored to peace.

The first day he had to repeat that process almost a hundred times. The next day it was only ninety times. And after many years, such outbursts almost never occurred. In

136

fact, he has actually been known to laugh when someone cuts him off in traffic—particularly if they are driving a little red sports car. Today, he is a different man. If you don't believe it, ask his wife. Instead of a lifetime of marital conflict, they have a near perfect relationship—thanks to the ministry of the Holy Spirit.

Anyone who knows the pastor will tell you he is a different person today. I can certainly testify to this, for you see, I am that man!

Anger is a subtle sin—particularly for men because it appeals to their "macho" complex. Most men think it is an expression of manhood. It is not! It is an expression of selfish pride, the root sin, and should have no place in the life of a Christian. I have found twenty-seven verses in the Bible that condemn it, verses like Psalms 37:8: "Cease from anger and forsake wrath."

You may respond, "but the Bible approves anger," or as some people tell me, "Jesus Himself was angry." Yes, there is a justifiable anger at sin, but it is defined by Paul in Ephesians 4:26 as an anger in which you do not sin. You don't permit it to exist beyond sundown, and even then, you watch yourself, or you will be vulnerable to temptation from the devil. We call this kind of anger "righteous indignation." The Savior was righteously indignant at the way the Jews were defaming the temple, so He drove them out. This was objective anger for something or someone other than himself. Later when He was reviled and persecuted, He did not get angry. Instead He responded, "Father, forgive them, for they know not what they do." That kind of indignation does not make you bleed inside; it never prompts you to explode in wrath. It is "righteous" indignation.

The anger the Bible condemns is the one most of us are confronted with every day—anger based on selfishness. Someone offends us or violates our rights, and we respond in selfish-induced anger—a sin that grieves the Holy Spirit and sets us up for spiritual defeat.

Discovering the fact that anger "grieves the Holy Spirit" and that it can be overcome was the greatest discovery of my life. Facing anger as sin and then confessing it whenever it raises its ugly head has changed my life.

Erwin W. Lutzer

Providential Parking Place

As the senior pastor of Moody Church in Chicago, Dr. Erwin W. Lutzer is one of God's chosen men to continue a great ministry begun by its founder Dwight L. Moody, one of the great Christian leaders of the centuries. Whenever I meet leaders associated with Moody, I am immediately impressed.

A former assistant professor of Bible and Theology at the Moody Bible Institute, Dr. Lutzer is the featured speaker on "The Moody Church Hour" and on the popular evening program, "Songs in the Night."

Dr. Lutzer is the author of numerous books, including Failure: The Back Door to Success, Managing Your

Emotions, Putting Your Past Behind You *and* All One Body: Why Don't We Agree?

Through Dr. Lutzer's story you will see how God works in even the smallest details of our lives to accomplish His will.

On April 3, 1977, my wife Rebecca and I were without a home church. The previous week had been my last as pastor of Edgewater Baptist Church in Chicago. I had resigned to devote time to my graduate studies and teaching at Moody Bible Institute. Since I had come to know Dr. Warren Wiersbe, the pastor of Moody Memorial Church, my wife and I, along with our children, drove from our suburban home to attend the church's morning worship service for the first time.

When we arrived, there were no parking spaces, so I left my wife and children at the church while I parked the car. To my delight, I saw a man walk across the street to his car and drive away. Immediately, I backed into the space.

As agreed, my wife and I met in the lobby. We were surrounded by crowds preparing to enter the auditorium. As we were deciding which door to enter, Dr. Wiersbe walked past wearing his topcoat. When he brushed by, I put my hand on his shoulder. "Warren, what are you doing in the lobby? It's only ten minutes before the morning service!"

"Erwin Lutzer!" he exclaimed. "I'm sick and on my way home. Would you preach for me this morning?"

Dr. Wiersbe introduced me to his staff, and I quickly recalled an outline of a message I had preached recently. As I stood on the platform and looked over the large congregation, I said in my heart, "Lord, if they ever call me to be pastor here, I'll say yes!" though I didn't seriously think that would ever happen.

But happen it did.

The first piece in the puzzle took shape a few months later when Pastor Wiersbe began asking me to speak whenever he was on vacation or took a missionary trip. I was grateful for the opportunity to further develop my preaching ministry.

When Pastor Wiersbe resigned in June of 1978, a committee was formed to seek his replacement. Since I was quite young and content teaching at Moody Bible Institute, I was not immediately considered as a candidate. The elders did ask me, however, to be interim pastor, so I spoke on the Sundays when there was no candidate in the pulpit. The second piece of the puzzle had fallen into place.

Even though I knew there were many men in America more qualified, I had the growing feeling that God was grooming me for this responsibility. Week by week that conviction strengthened.

But Rebecca was absolutely convinced that God did not want me to become pastor of Moody Church. During our successful five-and-a-half-year ministry at Edgewater Baptist Church, I had often expressed to her how weary I was with the many details expected of a pastor. Furthermore, she felt we were too young and unqualified. And she knew I thoroughly enjoyed teaching at the Institute. My schedule allowed me to write during the summer and speak in various churches on weekends. This, Rebecca believed, was best suited for my gifts and temperament.

Despite this disagreement, our marriage continued to be harmonious and fulfilling. We agreed on almost everything and enjoyed the three precious children God had given us. Only the subject of Moody Church caused tension.

I respected Rebecca's assessment, but God had

141

planted Moody Church in my heart. God had led us there; we simply had to accept it. I would tell Rebecca, "Someday, I will be the pastor of Moody Church; it is as certain as the conclusion of a geometric theorem!"

Of course, I expected her to get used to the idea. But as the months progressed, she remained firm in her conviction. I had no idea how deeply she felt until I came home one evening to find her sitting on the couch, her right hand pressed against her bowed head. I assumed she had a migraine headache. But she kept repeating, "I can't believe it, I can't believe it. I thought I *knew* you!"

Suddenly I realized this was not simply a minor difference of opinion; it had become an unresolvable issue that threatened the unity of our marriage. I could not convince her that God was leading in this direction. When I reminded her of how He had providentially provided a parking space on our first visit to Moody Church, she dismissed it as a coincidence.

"God," she said, "wanted you to speak that Sunday and provide occasional pulpit supply, nothing more."

One day, the whole matter came into sharp focus. I faced an excruciating contradiction. On one hand, God's call to Moody Church was absolutely certain; indeed this was verified by the response of the leadership and the congregation at large. The pulpit committee had concluded that I was God's choice for the position.

On the other hand, I couldn't serve as long as Rebecca opposed my acceptance of this call. I walked over to the window, stared outside, and spoke audibly to God. "Lord, I know I have been called to Moody Church; I also know that I cannot accept as long as Rebecca is opposed." And in my anguish I added, "I have never knowingly disobeyed You before, but am I going to have to this time?"

That was one of the darkest days of our marriage. But

God began to use this conflict to teach us an important lesson about His providential guidance and faithfulness. I tried to understand why Rebecca, who loved the Lord so deeply, felt that Moody Church and its ministries were so formidable. As the days passed, God began to change her heart. By the time the committee extended a formal call for me to become the pastor, Rebecca had decided to trust my judgment and the Lord's leading through the congregation. But there was one more step in the process.

Though I began my duties on January 1, 1980, the installation service was on January 20. It was the most beautiful winter day in Chicago. The temperature was 42 degrees; the sun shone brightly. Even the sunshine seemed a further confirmation of God's leading. That evening I wrote these words in my diary:

> This day marks a highlight in my life. Dr. Walvoord and Dr. Sweeting each gave a good word. Even the weather was beautiful; the temperature is in the 40s with not one flake of snow on the ground. Lord, I am yours for whatever you desire! Grant me grace to minister with blessing!

In March of that year, Rebecca was asked to speak to a women's conference in Toronto. As she prepared, God healed her heart, dissipating the doubt and confusion by showing her that she could be free from the frustration she felt about my decision. She felt a sense of release and fulfillment as she shared about her own struggles and how God would help her be the pastor's wife she wanted to be.

In the past twelve years, she has been content with that decision. The reason I can serve with freedom and joy is because Rebecca stands at my side with her love and prayers.

Together we have learned that *God's providential guidance extends to all the details of our lives, even to a parking space!* If we had not decided to come to Moody that Sunday back in 1977; *if* that man had not pulled out on LaSalle Street at exactly the right moment; *if* I had been standing somewhere else in the church lobby—*if* any one of these "ifs" had not happened, I would not be the pastor of Moody Church today. God gave me great liberty as I preached that morning, and He set the chain of events in motion that led to my call.

A corollary to the lesson of His providential guidance is that *when He calls, He enables*. God does not leave us without the resources to do His will. No matter how difficult obedience is, in the end, He will cause us to prevail.

Throughout the years, whenever I've been discouraged or faced inevitable disappointments in the ministry, I point to God's providential care as a reminder that the One who called me will be with me, no matter what. Frequently, I have had a great sense of release when I remind myself that the decision to become the senior pastor of Moody Church was His, not mine!

Though God gives His enabling each day, some examples stand out in my memory. On January 15, 1986, an arsonist broke into the church and set the organ, piano and pulpit furniture on fire, causing extensive damage. But the cleaning and refurbishing projects were so successful that it was hard to regret what had happened. Today our auditorium, instruments and equipment are better than ever. What is more, God used this event to unify the congregation and renew our sense of mission.

On April 20, 1990, the press criticized Moody Church because of a temporary decision regarding a child with AIDS in our Sunday school. Though I woke up that morning unable to get out of bed because of severe dizziness, through prayer I was raised up to clarify the matter at a press conference at 2 o'clock that afternoon.

In these and a hundred other instances, I have learned that the God who chose a parking place for me is the God who chooses the challenges that come each day. "Faithful is He who calls you, and He also will bring it to pass" (1 Thessalonians 5:24, NASB).

Bailey
Marks

Learning About
Faith From
a Hospital Bed

Dr. Bailey Marks was president of a prestigious, successful business when God led him and his wife Elizabeth to join the staff of Campus Crusade for Christ in 1967. Now he serves as the international vice president of our ministry, and it gives me tremendous joy and delight to work side by side with him in helping take the "most joyful news ever announced" to the ends of the earth.

In 1985 Bailey gave leadership to Explo '85, the world's largest satellite conference on evangelism and discipleship in history. Through eighteen satellites, every square inch of planet Earth was covered. More than 250,000 delegates from 164 countries participated in one week of training in discipleship and evangelism. Few men of our time have been so mightily used by God to help reach so many millions for Christ as Bailey.

You will be inspired to hear how God used a serious illness to help Bailey learn how to trust Him for the impossible—and how he applied this lesson to plan this worldwide conference that others thought could not be done.

"Look at all the things I gave up to serve you . . . and the way You treat *me* in return!"

These bitter thoughts tugged angrily at my heart as I lay on my hospital bed in San Bernardino, California. It was January 1969. As director of Asia and the South Pacific for Campus Crusade for Christ, I had recently returned from an extensive two-month trip into the area of my assignment. When I returned home just before Christmas, I felt very ill. Little did I know that I was dying a little bit each day; my liver was hardening and closing down.

Three years earlier my wife Elizabeth and I had left a lucrative position in business to take a more active part in helping to fulfill the Great Commission with Campus Crusade for Christ—a lot of responsibility for a relatively young Christian. Shortly after Elizabeth and I agreed that God wanted us to accept this opportunity, I became ill.

The doctors could not diagnose my problem, so I stayed in a hospital bed for a month, two and a half of those weeks in isolation. Everyone I saw was suited in full surgical attire, including Elizabeth who was only allowed to visit thirty minutes each day.

147

As I lay in that bed, I acted spiritual. Day after day people would telephone me and close their conversations by saying how much of a blessing I was to them. But one day I could no longer keep up the facade.

Putting down the receiver, I began to cry. Lonely, fearful and lying on that hospital bed far from my new field of service for my Lord—and dying—I couldn't understand why He had let me down. I felt like a fraud and a hypocrite for offering words of encouragement and blessing to others when inside I was angry and bitter at God. What I did not realize, of course, was that I was right where He wanted me, and I was about to learn one of the greatest lessons of my life.

I wanted to be a man of faith. I had not left my business to play games; I wanted to make an impact for God. Yet I had been play-acting with Him. Now that God had my attention, I began to ponder the whole matter of faith in the life of a believer.

I began to ask myself, "What is faith?" I recalled Hebrews 11:1: "Now faith is the assurance of things hoped for, the conviction of things not seen" (NASB). In other words, faith is confidence in God's holy Word and in His faithfulness.

Faith is not accidental, nor does it happen by osmosis. I must mentally decide that I am going to place my trust in God for my life or even for something that I feel He desires me to do. The decision is always mine, requiring an act of the will.

The synonym for faith is belief—to trust in something or someone to the extent that you know they will do what they say they will do. The antonym is unbelief. Somehow I thought that while faith required an action on my part, belief was passive and did not. So what about unbelief? It, in my opinion, required even less action. This was not correct.

Then while reading *God Unlimited* by Norman Grubb,

148

I saw a word I had never noticed before—"unfaith." I began to realize that, if faith required an act of my will, then "unfaith" did also. So, in reality, I had decided that I was not going to believe God for my situation.

Finally I understood that every aspect of my life—faith or unfaith, belief or unbelief—requires a mental decision on my part. The question is: Am I willing to place my confidence in God? Sometimes, I must admit, subconsciously I am not willing. Then I face a struggle which results in restlessness or lack of peace.

To exercise faith, however, I must come to grips with reality. First, I must get honest with myself and God and recognize my lack of faith for the situation I am facing. Second, I must say, "Lord, I am willing to believe You and Your promises."

That day in the hospital, I told the Lord I knew He cared for me and knew what was best for me and that I was willing to be sick and frail if that was His will.

The moment I began to be honest with myself and with God, things began to happen. My spiritual condition changed immediately, and my physical condition also began to improve. The doctors finally performed surgery and corrected the situation. Rather than taking six months to a year to get back on my feet as the doctors had expected, I was traveling within three months. In less than a year, Elizabeth and I moved our family to the Orient. And I have lived the last twenty-plus years quite successfully with a crippled liver and dietary supplements.

But the illness is not what is important. It is merely what God allowed me to go through so He could teach me one of the most important lessons I have ever learned: that faith takes an act of the will.

Since then, I cannot estimate the number of times I have had to apply this lesson. Subconsciously, it must be many times a day. And I have consciously had to work myself through countless difficult and faith-stretching situations—always with great blessing.

Over the next thirteen years, I saw God do many marvelous things, one of which was to see our full-time staff grow from ninety in nine countries to more than 2,700 in forty-four countries. I believe that and much more happened because I had decided to make active faith predominant in my life.

In 1983, after returning to the United States for two years, I took up my present position as executive vice president of our International Ministries. About that time, I was challenged by Bill Bright to plan for a worldwide training conference of about 30,000 students. Immediately, we realized that the cost was prohibitive.

But a worldwide conference could help accelerate our ministry throughout the world. So I continued to ask God for His direction. When it came, I was not prepared. In a rather unusual way, the Lord gave me the vision for a worldwide satellite conference which would take training to hundreds of thousands of conferees in many places around the world, rather than bring the 30,000 to one location.

To do something of this magnitude involved sophisticated technology that was totally foreign to me. Not only was I responsible for the conference and all the satellite aspects, but for the fund raising as well. I felt apprehensive, frightened and concerned about my personal reputation should the project fail. As a man of faith, I had been required to believe God for a lot of big things, but this was *really* big.

I could not say no to this challenge since that would have been "unfaith" to me. I had to get honest with myself and say to the Lord, "Help! I'm frightened and filled with doubts." I told Him I believed this was in accordance with His will and that I would exercise faith rather than unfaith.

BAILEY MARKS

EXPLO '85 became a reality in December 1985. More than 250,000 students and lay people—instead of the expected 30,000—attended in ninety-three locations around the world at a fraction of the original estimated cost! Each day, all were linked simultaneously by satellite. Miracle after miracle took place as God blessed in the lives of the conferees.

The benefits we experienced and continue to see in Campus Crusade are numerous. But the point is that I exercised my will to believe God in faith.

Trusting God in difficult situations is still not easy for me. But my prayer is that I will always be a strong, courageous, bold man—acting on my will to believe Him for the impossible.

Josh McDowell

Learning Servanthood the Hard Way

As a member of the Campus Crusade for Christ family for more than twenty-five years, Josh McDowell is one of the most articulate and popular youth speakers today. He has endeared himself to me and to thousands of our staff and millions of students and laymen. He truly is one of God's anointed men for the times in which we live.

Josh is the author or co-author of more than forty books and has been featured in twenty-six films, two television specials, an ongoing television series, and a weekly radio program.

His Why Wait? campaign has been used of God to

reach out to thousands of youth who want biblical answers to sexual questions.

Two of his books, Evidence That Demands a Verdict *and* More Than a Carpenter, *have become modern classics in defending the Christian faith.*

Josh shares how he grappled with resentment in learning the meaning of servanthood. Each of us can identify with the painful lessons he learned. You will enjoy reading about how he finally came to accept the role of a servant.

I felt so unappreciated. Once again I was put in charge of food at a student conference day of witnessing. Have you ever made 1000 peanut butter and jelly sandwiches? The more I made, the madder I got. Out of frustration I stuck the *Four Spiritual Laws* booklet inside a number of sandwiches between the peanut butter and jelly.

I wanted to be used by God. It was my dream to be a traveling speaker. How I wanted to teach His Word!

I was a graduate of Talbot Theological Seminary, had been on staff with Campus Crusade for four years, and yet had not given a talk or taught a seminar at a conference. All I had ever done was administrate and take care of the book table. When the staff took students to the beach witnessing, I was put in charge of transportation—and making all the sandwiches.

No one seemed to realize who I was—a seminary graduate and a speaker. They didn't understand what they had, so I thought. A sense of resentment developed in me toward Campus Crusade.

Then, suddenly, my hour of glory came. I got a call

from Ted Martin of Campus Crusade's Institute of Biblical Studies to teach at the IBS meetings later that year! I couldn't believe it! I had gone from nothing to everything all at once.

I prepared thoroughly for nearly six months. I planned to teach a series from the book of Romans and, when it was nearly time for the IBS meetings, had a wealth of notes and materials. I was looking forward to this teaching opportunity.

A week before IBS, I got a phone call from Bill Bright in California. "This is a special year for us at staff training at Arrowhead Springs," he said. "It's our international year, and we'll be having the largest number of staff ever. Josh . . . the administration at our hotel has fallen apart. I need you to help me. Please make arrangements right away. I'd like you to be back here in three days to take charge of the summer staff."

There was a pause on my end of the line. I had been looking forward to teaching at IBS. *What an abominable sense of timing,* I thought. *I don't want to go!*

"Josh, I need you," Bill Bright repeated.

"Okay . . . I'll be there."

Angrily, I threw my clothes and books together and packed them into the car. I fumed all the way to California, and my attitude hadn't improved when I arrived.

My assignment was to supervise the thirty staff people and organize the facilities for the nearly 1,700 people from all parts of the world. I stayed up all night the first few days putting together procedures and organization, trying to establish a basic administrative plan to handle the logistics of the hundreds of internationals expected.

But my inexperienced staff of thirty was no match for 1,700 incoming people—many of whom had trouble with English. Some had customs regarding meals and housing which were at odds with the best laid plans. To make matters

154

worse, the hotel's equipment broke down periodically—never when it was convenient and always when it caused even further disruption.

Finally, the proverbial straw. A terrible case of dysentery broke out. The sickness spread in a matter of two or three days to just about everyone. There were lines at every rest room, which were overworked to the point of breakdown as well.

I found myself—with bucket, mop and toilet plunger in hand—making the rounds of the rest rooms. The rest of the staff were either sick or tied up with the needs of preparing meals and other chores.

I was sick, too, but had no time to think about it. Every toilet in the hotel and in the other buildings had to be scrubbed twice a day. I worked twenty to twenty-two hours a day, able to catch only cat naps of two or three hours a night.

Somehow it all got done. But I had not been able to attend a single meeting to hear any of the world-famous speakers brought in for the occasion. I did meet one of them, however.

One day after I had just finished with the toilets on the second floor and had filled my bucket with fresh water, I picked up a plunger and started down the stairs to the lobby. I ran into Bill Bright escorting Billy Graham on a tour of the facilities. "Oh, Dr. Graham," he paused, waving to me, "I'd like you to meet our Canadian director, Josh McDowell."

The tall evangelist smiled graciously and stuck out his hand. This was my dream come true, and I wasn't going to miss the opportunity, at least, to shake his hand.

I awkwardly stuck the plunger under my arm, took the bucket in my left hand, wiped my right hand on my shirt, and sheepishly shook hands with Billy Graham.

As they walked away, Bill Bright remarked, "You

know, our staff people are devoted. They're willing to do anything."

I wanted to shout after them, "I'm not willing!"

The next afternoon, I finally finished vacuuming the brand new red carpet in the lobby, which was my last chore before I could go to hear Dr. Graham speak. At long last I'd be able to participate in one of the meetings which had been so encouraging for others.

Then Bill Bright rushed up to me. "Come here—quickly!" He pointed to the cleaned carpet. Footprints were visible across the length of the lobby. The parking lot had just been tarred, and someone had obviously tracked in the thick, tacky tar. "Get something—some cleaner, some rags. Hurry and clean it up before it sets."

It took all afternoon and most of the night to clean up the tar. The more cleaning solvent I rubbed into each spot, the bigger it got. That in turn called for more scrubbing—hard scrubbing.

A staff person came by just as I was finishing and teased me. "Scrub harder, slave! I still see some spots."

He was joking, but I was obviously in no mood for humor. I was ready to throw in the towel—literally. Angrily, I stood, all set to heave the solvent can at the front desk and scream out my resignation. Somehow the urge was checked.

Sudden conviction came over me. No one was really out to get me. I had brought an attitude of bitterness with me from Canada.

I recalled the Scriptures I had read in devotions that morning describing how Jesus washed the feet of the disciples. The thought pierced me: *If Jesus can wash the apostles' feet, why can't I scrub the staff's floors and clean their toilets?* It was an immediate lesson in submission.

That night I prayed for grace to be a true servant for

Christ. I realized that before I could ever become a leader I needed to learn how to be a follower. And the next day, I began a new pattern of service. I went out of my way to find things that needed doing; I worked harder and later than anyone else. It was something I wanted to do as a service to Christ to make up for getting off on the wrong foot. For the next several weeks, I fervently scrubbed and cleaned.

This willing spirit was not lost to others. Bill Bright said sympathetically, "God can teach us many things in a servant's role. When we first started, there were so many valuable things I learned by washing dishes, planting flowers, mowing the lawns—and yes," he laughed, "even scrubbing latrines."

It was difficult to continue the backbreaking responsibility of the six-week international staff training. Because of the work, sleeplessness and sickness, I lost more than twenty pounds.

I also found it difficult to measure the progress in my quest for submission and the attitude of a servant.

My first question was, *What can a person learn through servanthood?* Was Bill Bright merely trying to sound spiritual by indicating that God teaches through submission?

Second, I wondered, *Sure, the Lord said, "The greatest shall be the least," but wouldn't it be better to use your abilities for God in an aggressive, leadership capacity?* I thought the church lacked capable leaders and wondered if it was right to constantly put myself in the subservient role.

But everything I heard from Christian leaders, plus what I read about the subject in the Bible, all pointed to that earlier conviction—that God honors the servant and promotes the one who defers to others.

Not one easily learned, it is a lesson to consider again and again.

Patrick M. Morley

The God We Want Versus the God Who Is

Pat Morley endeared himself to me many years ago when I spoke at a Thanksgiving Prayer Breakfast in Orlando, Florida, an annual event for which he has served as chairman since its inception in 1978. He is an outstanding business and community leader who conducts a weekly Bible study with 125 key executives.

Pat founded Morley Properties Inc., which grew to be one of Florida's one hundred largest privately held companies. He has received several honors, including selection as an Outstanding Young Man of America by the U.S. Jaycees.

His bestselling book, The Man in the Mirror,

received the 1990 Gold Medallion Achievement Award in the Christian Living category. His I Surrender *is also making history.*

I am particularly impressed with Pat's desire to seek first the kingdom of God. Recently he announced that he and his wife Patsy will be leaving the business world to enter full-time Christian ministry.

Pat truly loves Christ. It has been my privilege to see him operate as a keen, astute businessman as a valued member of the board of directors of Campus Crusade for Christ.

In reading his story, you will learn how he tried to fit the Bible into his own plans and discovered the disastrous results of being a cultural Christian instead of a biblical believer.

The silent hush of the pre-dawn darkness filled our home as I tiptoed through the house. Taking my seat at the kitchen table, I began to read the new Bible my wife had given me as a gift. I treasured those moments sitting quietly alone— reading, thinking, studying, meditating.

Soon I began to underline the passages which particularly registered with me, the ones that seemed to favor the direction in which I was maneuvering my life. When such a morsel of Scripture was found, I memorized it.

At the same time, when I spotted a passage of Scripture which ran counter to my plans, I would pull out a large mental eraser and figuratively smudge that verse right off the page.

One morning I discovered an especially troubling text: "Do not be a man who strikes hands in pledge or puts up security for debts; if you lack the means to pay, your very bed will be snatched from under you" (Proverbs 22:26,27, NIV).

This was not the truth I was looking for. In fact, to follow this principle would stop all of my plans dead in their tracks. I was building a real estate business, and everyone knows you can't do that without mortgage debt. That required personal liability—meaning that *all* my assets were pledged to repay the debt, not just the asset against which the money was borrowed.

I tried everything to dilute the meaning of that verse. *Well, it's not a command*, I decided, *only a principle . . . It doesn't say I "will" have my bed snatched; it only says so if I can't pay. I'm smarter than the average Joe . . . I will be able to pay. This applies to a different time and place. Our laws don't permit losing everything—"my very bed." The risks are different today.*

Oh, how I wished I had never seen that verse! It tortured my mind. God had spoken directly to me, but the best real estate deals all seemed to require personal liability. Then one day, when my resistance was low, I crossed the line and struck my hand in pledge. After that I signed regularly.

The whole problem, of course, was that my approach was man-centered, not God-centered. Instead of earnestly seeking God's agenda, I was zealously trying to help God discover my agenda.

Looking back, I see how easily I had slid into this position . . .

When I became a Christian, I sincerely did receive Christ as Savior and Lord. Yet, in many ways, I just "added" Him to my life as another interest in an already busy and otherwise overcrowded schedule. I confess that many times I was more interested in the *benefits* of Jesus than in Jesus.

Slowly, I began to realize that there was not a one-to-one correlation between my *beliefs* and my *behavior*. I seemed to be Christian in spirit, but often secular in practice. Don't misunderstand—I was sincerely striving to be a moral, honest person. Oswald Chambers captured the crux of my problem when he wrote: "The majority of people have their morality well within their own grasp, they have no sense of the need of the gospel." Yet I had this lingering feeling that something wasn't quite right about my life. I was trying to have my cake and eat it too. I was living by a Christian life view part of the time, but I often formed plans, set priorities, solved problems, and made decisions in ways which reflected secular thinking.

In other words, I *syncretized* my life. I *added* Christian values and beliefs, but didn't *subtract* secular thinking. The result? Both Christian and secular ideas competed for control of the way I made decisions.

To put it another way—I became a *cultural Christian.* I pursued the God I wanted, but did not really know the God who is. I wanted Him to be a gentle grandfather who would spoil me and let me have my own way. I found myself following the God I was underlining in my Bible. In short, I created a fifth gospel: Matthew, Mark, Luke, John and Patrick.

Frankly, I did not intentionally or consciously set out to edit the Bible into my own version. Nevertheless, subtly, over time, through self-deceit and compromise, I "shoe-horned" the Word of God (like the Proverbs passage on striking hands in pledge) into my plans.

My entire life was built around the principle of *plan, then pray.* In other words, I knew where I was going and worked diligently to push my plans through to gain the necessary approvals from "headquarters."

I ignored the biblical command of Jesus which says, "If anyone would come after me, he must deny himself and take up his cross and follow me" (Matthew 16:24, NIV). Instead, I denied myself little.

One day it occurred to me that there simply wasn't much difference between my lifestyle and the lifestyles of those who made no claim of having Christ in their lives. I began to despise my life. Instead of offering hope to a broken, hurting world, I was devoting my energies to my own plans—ones devised to let me stand at center stage for a few brief moments.

I longed to change my life—to be salt and light. But a caldron of selfish ambitions bubbled, seethed, and boiled within me. Like a tug-of-war, they pulled me in the other direction. For several years I wrestled daily with the compromises that had infiltrated my life.

Then one day the big idea finally struck me: There is a God we want, and there is a God who is—but they are not the same God. Nothing we think, say, or do can make God into someone He is not. God is who He is, and He is unchanging as He proclaims, "I the Lord do not change" (Malachi 3:6, NIV).

One morning in early 1986, the truth finally connected with my brain: "The world and its desires pass away, but the man who does the will of God lives forever" (1 John 2:17, NIV). So, after two and one-half years of struggling to understand what had happened to me, I surrendered. On the title page of my Bible I wrote, "I want to spend the rest of my earthly life for the will of God." It was my turning point.

The lesson I learned is profoundly simple: When we stop seeking the God we want, we can start seeking the God who is. Jeremiah explains, "'You will seek me and find me when you seek me with all your heart. I will be found by you,' declares the LORD" (Jeremiah 29:13,14, NIV).

This turning point was the active choice to stop being a cultural Christian and to become a biblical Christian. And this commitment includes the decision to approach the Scriptures objectively, instead of looking for evidence to support the choices already made. It is the decision to *pray, then plan.* And it is the greatest lesson I have ever learned.

Lloyd J. Ogilvie

The Secret of
True Power

Dr. Lloyd J. Ogilvie is pastor of the historic First Presbyterian Church in Hollywood, California, where I received Jesus Christ as my Savior and Lord more than forty-five years ago. He hosts the nationally syndicated radio and television ministry "Let God Love You." The program began twelve years ago with one television station in Los Angeles and is now seen throughout the nation on independent stations and cable networks.

Dr. Ogilvie is the author of many books, including the daily devotional Silent Strength and Making Stress Work For You, winner of a Gold Medallion Book Award. He also served as general editor of the thirty-two-volume Communicator's Commentary.

LLOYD J. OGILVIE

*Dr. Ogilvie is in great demand as a speaker for con-
ventions, conferences, and renewal retreats for clergy and
laity. He is truly one of God's anointed, Spirit-filled servants,
who always ministers to my heart whenever I hear him speak.*

*Here Dr. Ogilvie describes how he caught a vision of
what a Christian is meant to be. This secret led him to a new
boldness and joy and changed his ministry dramatically.*

It was the last day of the prolonged, solitary retreat I
had taken on a lonely beach during the summer after my first
year as a Presbyterian pastor. I took a stick and wrote in the
firm sand all of my needs, yearnings and failures. Then I
scratched out a list of the sad results of a powerless life and
ministry. Though it was many years ago, I can remember that
time as if it happened today . . .

I'd been a Christian for eight years. With seminary
and post-graduate studies completed, I began my ordained
ministry. My preaching was biblically sound and Christ-
centered, and I taught good orthodox reformed theology. As
a man "in Christ," I knew I was a recipient of salvation
through the gift of His death and resurrection. I knew I was
forgiven, that death had no power over me and that I was
alive forever. I tried to follow Christ to the best of my ability.
Yet, I still had a problem.

Few lives were moved or changed as a result of my
ministry. Something was wrong; something was lacking.
Depending on human energy, talents and personality, I had
no power for a supernatural ministry. Popularity and out-
ward success did not satisfy my gnawing, inner spiritual
hunger—a real need and longing for authentic power. As a
result, I became exhausted and frustrated.

165

This led me to my solitary retreat. I was alone with Christ, and He guided me to spend the time studying the Gospel of John, chapters 14, 15, 16, along with Paul's letter to the Colossians.

Again and again, I stumbled over the Lord's words, "Apart from me, you can do nothing" (John 15:5, NIV). The words contradicted my aggressive, self-assertive addiction to human power. Repeatedly, I read Christ's promise that He would make His home in me, and I longed to experience His presence. Then I read these words in Colossians, "Christ in you, the hope of glory" (Colossians 1:27, NIV). They sounded like the blast of a trumpet.

"That's it!" I exclaimed. Suddenly, I had caught a vision of what a Christian is meant to be—the resurrection home of the risen Christ.

During those days, the secret of true power became real to me. The pre-existent, reigning, all-powerful Christ is also the indwelling Lord. The glory promised was a manifestation of Christ in me, a character transplant so that I could be like Him in attitude, action and reaction. A liberating conviction captured my mind: *Christianity is not only life as Christ lived it; it is more than my life in Him; it is Christ living in me!*

I had read those Scriptures before. How had I missed the experience of these promises? The Lord wanted a surrender of all there was of me—mind, soul, will, and body—to Him. It took the crisis of powerlessness to make me ready to receive what was offered all along.

I got on my knees and asked Christ to indwell my total life. I prayed, "Lord, I've missed the secret. I've been ministering for You and have not allowed You to work through me. Come live Your life in me. I am empty and need to be filled. Love through me; care through me; preach

166

through me; lead through me. All that I am or ever hope to be, I yield to You."

Christ's presence flooded my entire being, from the top of my head to the soles of my feet. I felt loved, forgiven, empowered. I don't know how long I was on my knees, but it must have been a long time because when I got up the tide had come in and washed away all I had written in the sand.

I returned home a different person, set free from my compulsive efforts to try to earn my status with the Lord. The experience replenished the parched places of my soul that had kept my Christian life a constant dry spell. The indwelling Christ gave me all that I had previously worked so hard to achieve, studied to understand, struggled to accomplish. Now I was free to love without restraint and felt a new boldness, an exuberant joyousness I couldn't contain.

One of the greatest changes was in my preaching. Instead of depending on human talent, rhetoric and scholarship alone, I experienced wisdom beyond my understanding, knowledge beyond my learning, and discernment beyond my insight. I was amazed. Only Christ could have given me these gifts, and I give Him all the glory.

I began to preach each sermon as if never to preach again. The secret of true power that had been missing in my life and message, the power of the indwelling Christ, became the thrust of my preaching. My new theme was that nothing can happen *through* us until it happens *to* us. And there is no limit to what Christ will do in us if we yield our lives as a laboratory in which we discover what He wants to share with others through us.

But don't misread my enthusiasm for what happened so many years ago. It has had to be renewed every day, especially in each new challenge or difficulty. I have known my share of suffering and pain, disappointments and problems. And I've been called to attempt some humanly impossible tasks. Looking back, I can't imagine living through it all without the power of the indwelling Christ.

Over the years, the resiliency of His presence has given me a tireless expectancy. I've discovered that guidance is not something I must beg to receive, but something Christ signals within my mind and spirit. My task is only to pray for openness to let Him through, and then to marvel at what He says and does. Then each person I meet or work with gives me a fresh opportunity to let go and allow Christ to speak or love through me.

What a relief it is to no longer feel that I have to find answers and solve problems on my own! He is at work in me. I know that as surely as I feel my heart beat and my lungs breathe. Problems and difficulties are really gifts for new levels of depth in experiencing the limitless adequacy of what Christ can do.

And I know something else. We are meant to be riverbeds for the flow of His Spirit, not reservoirs. Christ's indwelling power is for servanthood, not for private, esoteric piety. When Christ takes up residency in us, He leads us into situations and to people who need Him most. And the more we serve, the more power He releases.

When I was asked to share my most beneficial lesson, my mind was flooded by magnificent things I've discovered in the trials and triumphs through the years. At first, it was difficult to select one that was the *most* beneficial. And then it hit me—all the experiences of growth through the years were but diminutive repetitions of the ultimate discovery there on the lonely beach where I was not alone. And each one brought me back to a renewal of the secret of the abundant life I experienced—that Christ in your heart is your only hope of glory.

Luis
Palau

———⬥⬥⬥———

Any Old Bush
Will Do

Luis Palau is one of the great evangelists of our time. During more than twenty years of ministry, he has spoken in person to more than nine million people in almost sixty nations and to many more millions through his radio and television broadcasts.

Luis began his evangelistic career at the age of eighteen, preaching on weekends while he worked at an Argentine bank. Within a few years, he and several other young men organized a tent evangelism and radio ministry in Argentina.

Since that time, his ministry has continued to flourish. God has used him to bring multitudes to Jesus Christ in Central and South America, North America, Europe, the

South Pacific, Asia, Africa and the Soviet Union. Convinced of his love for our Lord and demonstrated integrity, I consider it a special delight, along with members of our staff, to cooperate with him in his various crusades.

In his account, Luis shows how he learned to depend on Christ alone. His story begins in his late teenage years with his search for a holy life.

Whenever a great preacher came to our church in Argentina, some of my friends and I would try to get an interview with him. Our questions were always the same. "How can we get victory over temptation? How can we live holy lives?"

Usually the visiting preacher would ask, "Are you reading the Bible?"

"Yes, we get up at five every morning before going to school or work. We read several chapters every day."

"Great! But are you testifying for Jesus?"

"Yes. We hand out tracts, teach children's classes, and even hold street meetings."

"That's terrific! But are you praying?" the preacher would ask. So we'd tell him about our all-night prayer meetings.

Our frustration must have been obvious. "What else do we need to do?" we'd ask.

"Well, pray some more, witness some more, read the Bible some more." So we did. And we just about killed ourselves, we were so eager to be holy.

I was on the verge of giving up, not because I saw a

lack in God, but because I was weary of fighting and strug-gling and seeking on my own to persevere through sheer dedication.

When am I ever going to catch on? I wondered. *Will I give up now, after all I've been through?* I wanted to please and love and serve God. I wanted people to be saved. I would sing, "Oh, Jesus, I have promised to serve Thee to the end," and I would think, *even if it kills me.*

One day I was invited to view a brief film of Billy Graham speaking to Christian leaders in India. Although he spoke before an unbelievable crowd of tens of thousands, he seemed to be staring right into my eyes as he quoted Ephesians 5:18: "Do not get drunk on wine, which leads to debauchery. Instead, be filled with the Spirit" (NIV). It was as if the crowd in India didn't exist. He was looking right at me and shouting, "Are you filled with the Spirit?"

I knew that was my problem—I wasn't filled with the Holy Spirit. That was the reason for my up-and-down Chris-tianity. That's why I had zeal and commitment, but little fruit or victory. When would it end? When would I find the answer?

I found it in the United States after several frustrating months of Bible school.

I came to the States through the patient prodding of Ray Stedman, pastor of Peninsula Bible Church in Palo Alto, California. The first two months, I lived in his home. I was argumentative and wanted to discuss theology and doctrine for hours. I had come to learn, but maybe I wasn't yet ready to admit that I didn't have all the answers.

After two months with the Stedmans, I went to Multnomah School of the Bible in Portland, Oregon. Multnomah is a demanding school, and I found the first semester particularly rough.

Our Spiritual Life class professor, Dr. George Kehoe,

only added to my frustration when he began *every* class period by quoting Galatians 2:20: "I have been crucified with Christ, and I no longer live, but Christ lives in me. The life I live in the body, I live by faith in the Son of God, who loved me and gave himself for me" (NIV).

I was still frustrated in not being able to live the lifestyle I saw in men like Ray Stedman and several others at Peninsula Bible Church and at Multnomah. Their lives exhibited a joy and freedom that I found attractive. But the more I sought it, the more elusive it seemed.

My spiritual journey seemed like a climb up a tall cliff. I clawed every inch of the way only to slip and slide back down. Although I had experienced times of blessing and victory, for the most part I felt the struggle was impossible. I couldn't go on that way, especially when no one else knew about it. It was my secret, private death.

I felt like a hypocrite. If I were to describe myself in those days, I would have to say I was envious, jealous, too preoccupied and self-centered, and ambitious to a wrong degree. I was smug about other speakers, silently rating their illustrations or delivery against my own. That left me feeling mean and ugly and petty. No amount of wrestling with myself would rid me of those sins. And yet I tried. I felt despicable; I hated the idea that I was a hypocrite.

Maybe that's why I didn't like the constant reminder of Galatians 2:20 and was getting annoyed at Dr. Kehoe's quoting that verse every day. *It can't be a Bible verse that gets you so upset,* I told myself. *It must be you.* Rather than let that verse penetrate my pride, I decided that the verse was self-contradictory, hard to understand and confusing, especially in English.

Shortly before Christmas break, Major Ian Thomas, founder and director of Torchbearers, the group that runs Capernwray Bible School in England, spoke at our chapel service. I usually sat in the back of the auditorium and dared the speaker to make me pay attention. If he was good, I'd honor him by listening. Otherwise I would daydream or peek at my class notes.

Ian Thomas talked about Moses and how it took this great man forty years in the wilderness to learn that he was nothing. Then one day Moses was confronted with a burning bush—likely a dry bunch of ugly little sticks that had hardly developed—yet Moses had to take off his shoes. Why? Because this was holy ground. Why was it holy ground? Because God was in the bush!

Here was Major Thomas's point: God was telling Moses, "I don't need a pretty bush or an educated bush or an eloquent bush. *Any old bush will do, as long as I am in the bush.* If I am going to use you, I am going to use you. It will not be you doing something for Me, but Me doing something through you."

It suddenly hit me that I was that kind of bush: a worthless, useless bunch of dried-up sticks. I could do nothing for God. All my reading and studying, asking questions, and trying to model myself after others was worthless. Everything in my ministry was worthless, unless God was in the bush. Only He could make something happen.

Thomas told of many Christian workers who failed at first because they thought they had something to offer God. He himself had once imagined that because he was an aggressive, winsome, evangelistic sort, God would use him. But God didn't use him until he came to the end of himself. *That's exactly my situation,* I thought. *I am at the end of myself.*

Thomas closed his message by reading—you guessed it—Galatians 2:20. And then it all came together for me. "I have been crucified with Christ and *I no longer live, but Christ lives in me.*" My biggest spiritual struggle was finally over! I would let God be God and let Luis Palau be dependent upon Him.

I ran back to my room and in tears fell to my knees next to my bunk. "Lord, now I understand!" I prayed in my native Spanish. "The whole thing is 'not I, but Christ in me.' It's not what I'm going to do for You, but rather what You're going to do through me."

I stayed on my knees until lunchtime, an hour and a half later. I asked the Lord's forgiveness for my pride.

Well, God still had a lot of burning to do, but He was finally in control of this bush. He wanted me to be grateful for all the small things He had put in my life, but He didn't want me to place my confidence in those opportunities to make me a better minister or preacher. He wanted me to depend not on myself or my breaks, but on Christ alone—the indwelling, resurrected almighty Lord Jesus.

That day marked the intellectual turning point in my spiritual life. The practical working out of that discovery would be lengthy and painful, but at last the realization had come. We have everything we need when we have Jesus Christ living in us. It's His power that controls our dispositions, enables us to serve, and corrects and directs us (Philippians 2:13). I could relax and rest in Him. He was going to do the work through me.

Norman Vincent Peale

Experiencing the Positive Power of Christ

More than forty years ago as a young Christian, I was challenged in my walk with Christ by Dr. Norman Vincent Peale when he spoke at the First Presbyterian Church in Hollywood where I was a member. Through the years as I have come to know him better, his enthusiasm for our Savior continues to inspire me.

Some years ago, I was privileged to be invited to New York City for a special meeting with Dr. Peale and his wife

175

Ruth to plan a strategy to help reach America for Christ. I was deeply moved by his sincerity and desire to communicate the gospel of our Lord Jesus Christ with the entire country.

Dr. and Mrs. Peale are co-editors and publishers of the popular Guideposts *magazine. He has written thirty-nine books, including* The Power of Positive Thinking, *which has sold more than fifteen million copies. Dr. Peale also is the recipient of the Presidential Medal of Freedom.*

Dr. Peale's story is about a man who influenced his life in a dramatic way. The transformation in this man's life will inspire you to also experience—and share—the positive power of Christ.

Sometimes an event occurs in a person's life with dramatic suddenness, and as a result that person is never the same again.

The experience may penetrate so deeply into personality that it leaves a permanent impression. And that powerful effect can possibly change the individual for life.

Such an unforgettable and determinative experience happened to me one cold, February night when I was a small boy. It conditioned my thinking and living for a lifetime.

The snow lay deep around the white, steepled church in my little midwestern hometown. Light gleamed through the windows, welcoming the worshippers who struggled through the drifts to the door. Many, stamping off snow, entered the little church until it was filled to the last seat. Even more crowded in to stand.

The midwinter revival gatherings, which met every night for two weeks of evangelistic preaching, were called "protracted meetings." And the community's interest was intense—especially if the preacher, in this case my father, was well-known throughout the area as a powerful speaker motivated by a sincere faith and dedication to Jesus Christ.

Since in those days there was no radio or television to compete and, indeed, no motion picture theater, the church was the focal point of interest. A special series of revival meetings, long anticipated, attracted not only regular churchgoers, but the irregular and non-religious as well. Few ignored the enthusiasm generated as the meetings progressed night after night.

Present each night and sitting near the front with my mother and younger brother, Bob, I felt the excitement and awareness of God's presence that developed as the revival series mounted in zeal. The content was controlled emotionally, however, for my father was suspicious of the emotionalism that sometimes prevailed at such meetings and often resulted in a falling away of people converted superficially. What he wanted was in-depth life-change in which not only emotion but the mind combined in a commitment bringing spiritual growth and lifelong Christian discipleship. The anticipation of great things happening was in the air, and on one particular night something great did occur.

There was a man in the community, Dave Henderson, who was a rough, tough character. He would go on regular drunks. Nowadays he would be considered an alcoholic. His speech was profane, and he could easily be provoked into a fight. And he had a mean streak that was revealed in violent outbursts of temper. Rumor had it that he was a wife-beater, but his sweet and dignified mate never let on that he was anything but a perfect husband.

Despite everything, something about Dave was likable, and my father, a "he-man" type of minister, was rather fond of him. I recall his saying, "There is something pretty fine in that man if he would only let the Lord bring it out."

And Dave, in turn, liked my father. He would often come to church, sit in a rear pew, and afterward say to Father, "I like to hear you talk, Reverend." But still he went on with his lifestyle which most charitably could be described, to use words prevalent in those days, as "wicked and evil." He was the bad man of the town.

Then came the unforgettable night. The meeting opened with the congregational singing of old revival hymns. Prayer was offered, the Scriptures read. Then Father went into his sermon. He was always tender and loving— most persuasive. He loved Jesus, and that love communicated itself impressively to the congregation. He told how powerful and loving Jesus is—that the Savior can do the most wonderful things in even the worst lives. The sermon was thoughtful, intelligent and irrefutable in its logical presentation. And it was heightened by love. My father loved these people, and one by one, he had loved them into the Kingdom.

He finished his sermon by giving the invitation to all who wanted to be saved and know the Lord, to be converted and have their lives changed, to come forward to the altar and receive the power of Christ.

There was a moment of silence. Then I could almost feel the church shake a bit as a heavy man started down the aisle. Seated at the end of the pew, I looked back to see Dave walking with a kind of determined air, quite unconscious of the stir he was creating. Tears were streaming down his cheeks. Even though I was a small boy, I knew that this man was deeply moved.

Reaching the altar, Dave knelt. Father knelt with him and, as he later told us, said to him, "Dave, you have been struggling against God, and that is no good. God wants you, my dear friend, and if you surrender to Him, He will give you peace and joy, and your life will be wonderful forever."

178

Dave said quietly, "Reverend, I want Jesus. I can't do anything with my life. I don't want to be this way anymore."

Father put his hand on the big fellow's shoulder and said, "Receive Jesus Christ who forgives all your sins and makes you now His own."

I could not hear this conversation. It was spoken in low tones, and I report it here from memory as told to me by my father more than seventy years ago.

Then Dave rose and turned around to face the congregation, all of whom knew him for his bad qualities and actions. He said only, "Jesus! Thank You, Jesus!" But it was the look on his face that got me, and indeed, everyone else. It was a look that was other-worldly in its beauty. His countenance was transformed, illuminated. It was beautiful. It was so incredibly wonderful that tears welled up in my eyes. The feeling I had was one of wonderment, astonishment. How could this be? Surely this wasn't happening to *this* man! And just what was happening? The answer is that the positive power of Jesus Christ was happening. A man was being transformed.

And Dave was changed. Some people said it wouldn't last. But it did. From that moment, this man was totally different. He broke instantly with all his bad habits. He became a good, honorable, upright man of God. Literally, he became a saint—a rugged, loving saint. And if I were called upon to name the best men, the most Christ-like men I have ever known, Dave Henderson would be right up there at the top of the list.

But still, even though I was only a small boy, I was confused. How could this be—a man walks into a church one sort of man and leaves the church totally different? "What happened, Father?" I asked. "What happened to Dave in that one minute of time?"

Father smiled. "It's wonderful, Norman; it's all very

179

wonderful. The power happened to him. He received the power—the positive power of Jesus Christ. He is a new man in Christ."

I can recall to this day my father repeating that glorious line from Scripture: "If anyone is in Christ, he is a new creation; old things have passed away; behold, all things have become new" (2 Corinthians 5:17, NKJ). Then Father added, "The fact that Jesus Christ can do this to people made me a preacher."

And, I might add, it made me a preacher also.

So the years passed, and Dave kept the faith. He walked among men as a man of God. He was beloved, even venerated. He was a blessing to everyone he met. Eventually, his big head was crowned with snowy white hair. Love and kindness were written on his rugged countenance. Then he became ill, and I received word that the end was near. I immediately went from my home in New York back to the little town where he lived to see him once more. He lay in bed, his white hair against the pillow. His giant form was now emaciated. His big hand, now so thin, was white against the sheet, and the blue veins showed clearly. We talked of the old times, particularly of my father. "Greatest man I ever knew," said Dave. "He led me to Christ. And what greater thing can one man do for another?"

Then I asked Dave to pray for me. I knelt by the side of his bed and could feel his hand reaching for me. Presently, it rested on my head. I cannot now recall just what he said. I only know that this was a sacred experience. I felt cleansed and blessed. I felt the Holy Presence. It was one of the deepest and most beautiful spiritual experiences of my life.

Dennis
Rainey

―――――❦―――――

The Legacy of a
"Good Name"

Dennis Rainey is co-founder and director of Campus Crusade for Christ's Family Ministry in Little Rock, Arkansas. As a featured speaker for Family Life Conferences, he has ministered throughout the United States and Canada, as well as South Africa, South Korea and Singapore. He has also conducted marriage and family seminars for some of America's largest corporations.

As one of my associates, Dennis is being used of God to influence tens of thousands of families. I am always excited when he shares the heartwarming reports of couples who are inspired to make our Lord the center of their marriages after attending a Family Life Conference.

With his wife Barbara, Dennis is co-author of the

bestselling book, **Building Your Mate's Self-Esteem,** *and he has also authored* **Lonely Husbands, Lonely Wives** *and the HomeBuilders Couples Series study,* **Building Your Marriage.**

His story begins in a small town in Missouri with his first attempt as a salesman. Through this experience and others, Dennis shares the seed of his character development, the integrity of his father.

Growing up in a small, rural community nestled in the Ozark Mountains of southern Missouri meant there were few secrets. As a teenager, I learned that mistakes made on Saturday night were Monday morning's headline news at the local barber shop. It was generally true both for children and adults: An individual's character and reputation were like laundry hanging outdoors on the clothesline—there for all to see.

By the time I was a senior in high school, I had become acutely aware of the negative side of our little community's efficient communication network. However, I didn't realize it had its positive side until I began selling magazine subscriptions to raise money for our senior project.

As the contest began, I set my eyes on a small tape recorder and a teddy bear that would be my reward for selling a modest number of subscriptions. Without delay I cashed in several sales to my numerous aunts and uncles.

However, it became increasingly difficult as I solicited subscriptions from my neighbors. I was still a good distance from my goal when I found myself going door to door in town. That strategy didn't break any sales records, so I headed out into the country. There I met considerable resistance while burning a tank of gas. Sales had ceased.

As I was driving home about to give up and settle for a cheap, pint-sized, stuffed chipmunk, I impulsively turned off the gravel road into a driveway that led to a small, white farm house. As I got out of the car and walked up the steps, I thought to myself, *They probably can't afford to buy anyway.* My suspicions were inwardly confirmed when I was greeted by an elderly man in well-worn overalls standing behind the screened door.

I introduced myself and was hurriedly rattling off my canned sales pitch when the old man interrupted me: "Son, what did you say your name was?"

"Dennis Rainey, sir," I tried to say politely, wondering what that had to do with my sales presentation.

"Are you 'Hook' Rainey's son?" he asked with a slight grin.

The old man's etched face immediately brightened with my answer, "Why, yes sir. He's my dad."

"Well come on in!" He beamed as he unhooked the screen door and swung it open. He went on and on about my father, telling stories of how he had bought home heating fuel from Dad for years, how Dad had helped him and others when they couldn't pay their bills.

Then he bought two magazine subscriptions.

Driving away, I decided to see if this was a fluke or if others shared the same opinion about my dad. I stopped at the next little house on the edge of that country road and introduced myself. "Hello, I'm 'Hook' Rainey's son; my name is Dennis Rainey."

Eureka! The response was identical. Sales soared as I drove from house to house down every gravel road I could find. Not only did I win the tape recorder, but I also won thirteen huge stuffed animals—teddy bears, tigers and dogs. I cleaned them out by winning first place and setting a record for sales.

For years I thought *I* had won that magazine sales contest. But it wasn't until Dad's death that I realized what had happened: It was his character that had made the difference. I had witnessed a living Proverb:

> A good name is to be more desired than great riches (Proverbs 22:1, NASB).

My dad's good name was earned during sixty-six years lived within two miles of where he was born. His character was shaped as a boy when his father deserted him, his mother, and six other brothers and sisters. As a lad, Dad learned what it meant to be responsible as the family struggled to scratch out enough to feed eight in a two-room drafty log cabin.

During his late teenage years, he picked up his nickname "Hook." Evidently, in his prime he was a pretty fair baseball pitcher—he even pitched a game against Dizzy Dean. As a lefty, he was known for having the most crooked curve ball around—a wicked "hook" that mystified batters.

But in contrast to his curve ball, Dad's life was as straight and powerful as a Nolan Ryan fastball. He was widely known and known well in the business community. As a single man, he started his own business pumping gas and, over a forty-four-year period, built a solid company. At his funeral, attended by about a third of the town, one man commented, "I never heard a negative word about 'Hook' Rainey."

At the heart of Dad's good name was his integrity. His word was good. His promises were sealed with a firm handshake. No contracts were needed to make certain he didn't become slippery in business.

His commitment to my mom in 1932 was sure until his death in 1976.

He made good on his promises to me to go fishing during busy times of the year. I remember thinking as a young boy that if I could only get him to say yes to something, then it was a done deal. His integrity permeated all that he did; his private life was no different from his public life.

Dad was a man of few words. He had a soft-spoken faith in God, but underneath was a bedrock of practical righteousness. He wasn't perfect, but he was never pompously pious.

Upon reflection, I sometimes feel that my dad's life was a lesson in character and integrity—just for me. As I go about trusting my heavenly Father, His Word, and His plan for my life, I've learned that the seeds of trust were planted there by an earthly father who was trustworthy. I agree with Alexander Pope when he said, "An honest man is the noblest work of God." It is from observing this noble work of God that I draw strength daily to live my life and lead my family.

As I ponder the greatest lesson my dad taught me, I'm grateful to God for a father who embodied the words of Charles Haddon Spurgeon who said, "A good character is the best tombstone. Those who loved you and were helped by you, remember you when forget-me-nots are withered. Carve your name on hearts, and not on marble."

The older I become, the more I am grateful to God for a dad who engraved integrity upon his son's heart. I pray that I will do the same.

> Praise the Lord!
> How blessed is the man who fears the Lord.
> Who greatly delights in His commandments.
> His descendants will be mighty on earth;
> The generation of the upright will be blessed
>   (Psalm 112:1,2, NASB).

Adrian Rogers

The Souvenirs
of Pain

Adrian Rogers is pastor of the 20,000-member Bellevue Baptist Church of Memphis, Tennessee. He has served three terms as president of the Southern Baptist Convention.

Adrian and I first met more than twenty-five years ago when Campus Crusade for Christ conducted a Lay Institute for Evangelism in a church he was pastoring in Florida. We have continued our friendship, and through the years I have been tremendously impressed as he has powerfully proclaimed God's holy, inspired Word and faithfully exalted our Lord Jesus Christ, both in his personal life and his ministry.

Highly regarded as an evangelist and speaker, Adrian has taught in the Billy Graham Schools of Evangelism and held city-wide crusades in the United States and abroad. In 1980 he brought a major address to a gathering of more than 500,000 assembled for the "Washington for Jesus" rally.

His greatest lesson came through a tragedy in his family. He reminds us of how Jesus suffered and of how His scars are momentos of the pain He endured for us.

Often when we visit a place, we bring back a souvenir. It's our way of saying, "I've been there." Our Lord brought back some souvenirs from His journey to planet Earth—the scars that He bears in His glorified body.

Indeed, the only man-made things in heaven are the scars that Jesus bears. After His resurrection, those scars convinced Thomas that He indeed had risen (John 20:24-29). The glorified body that brought Thomas to his knees still had "the print of the nails."

Jesus was a suffering God. His scars are memorials of excruciating pain. They are eternal reminders to me of the greatest lesson I've ever learned: God is faithful and trustworthy to turn our scars into ministry to others.

The world today is having great difficulty with the problem of pain. Some agonize in a dungeon of doubt because of indescribable and seemingly senseless suffering. How often have you asked God to remove a problem, and it seemed to get worse? Why is this, if God is love and all-powerful?

Is it that God is love, but weak and powerless? Or that He is powerful, but without love and, therefore, cruel? Or even worse—is there no love or power because there is no God at all?

The answer to these questions lie in our response to an even greater issue. Can God suffer? Indeed, He can and does! And why does God Himself suffer?

Think about it. It's reasonable.

Does not a father suffer with his children? The story of the prodigal son is meant to teach, among other things, that a father suffers when his son does. We're told to "grieve not the Holy Spirit" (Ephesians 4:30, KJV). "Grieve" is a love word. We can only grieve someone who loves us. Your lawn mower may vex you, but your children can grieve you. Yes, our loving heavenly Father is often grieved for His children.

Does not the head feel and register pain coming in from a wounded body? Jesus is the exalted head of the church, which is His body, and He, therefore, continues to "be touched with the feeling of our infirmity" (Hebrews 4:15, KJV).

Does not a loving groom grieve if his betrothed bride is unfaithful or indifferent to him? Surely, the heavenly Bridegroom, Jesus, is heartbroken over the church which sometimes proves to be a faithless and fickle bride.

But why would God suffer? He is God. He could choose not to suffer. Yes, but He allows Himself to suffer, and that brings us to the next question.

Why doesn't God just remove pain? Because pain is an absolutely necessary commodity in a world that has been cursed by sin.

Pain is God's way to remind us that this universe in which we live has a disease, and we indeed are part of it. It is His loving reminder that mankind needs the healing of redemption. The apostle Paul explains, "We know that the whole creation groaneth and travaileth in pain together until now. And not only they, but ourselves also . . . groan within ourselves, waiting for the adoption, to wit, the redemption of our body" (Romans 8:22,23, KJV).

A loving God could not remove the pain (a result of

sin) until the last vestige of sin (the infection of our world) is dealt with and gone. The worst thing that could happen to fallen humanity would be to live blindly in "paradise" and never seek a Savior.

Thank God that our Lord does not remove pain. The scars, to the contrary, tell us that He shares the pain. Hebrews 4:15 assures us, "We have not an high priest which cannot be touched with the feeling of our infirmities; but was in all points tempted like as we are, yet without sin" (KJV).

The sad part is that we are a generation that blocks out pain at any cost. It's amazing what we have concocted to accomplish this: drugs, alcohol, sexual affairs, television and amusements. Many are merely heading for a sedative to kill the pain instead of coming to the Savior to heal the infection.

When we come to Jesus, He may not remove all of the pain because, though we have been saved from the penalty of sin, we still need to be saved from the presence of sin. Therefore, He may not remove the painful thorn, but gives added grace and joy to help us endure it (2 Corinthians 12:1-10).

Our Lord did not have to suffer, but He invaded our sufferings so He could bear them and heal them. The prophet Isaiah proclaims, "He was wounded for our transgressions, he was bruised for our iniquities; the chastisement of our peace was upon him; and with his stripes we are healed" (Isaiah 53:5, KJV). Because of Calvary, we're saved. Not only did He die, but He arose again and lives forever to wear the scars.

The great lesson in all of this for me is that Jesus has some scars, and so will we if we are to be like Him. The apostle Paul says, "From henceforth let no man trouble me: for I bear in my body the marks of the Lord Jesus" (Galatians 6:17, KJV).

Remember that a scar is a wound that has healed. *We*

189

need to bring our wounds to Jesus, let Him heal them, and then *use our scars for Jesus.*

Indeed, your scars may be your greatest ministry. Just as the scars of Jesus convinced Thomas, perhaps your scars will convince someone today.

After seminary, my wife Joyce and I were called back to Florida to a fine little church in Fort Pierce. By this time we had three children: Steve, Gayle and Philip. Philip was only two months old when we settled into the new parsonage.

It happened on Mother's Day. It was a beautiful day, as the days in May so often are near the Florida coast. I had just preached a Mother's Day message on the blessings of a Christian home. Our small house was nestled right next door to the little white, cement block church. Joyce was out in the kitchen preparing our lunch after the service. And I was in the living room reading.

Suddenly I heard her distraught voice. "Adrian! Come here quickly! Something is wrong with Philip."

I leaped to my feet. She had our baby boy in her arms. He was not breathing. His face had a blue cast to it.

"What's wrong?" she cried.

"I don't know. You call the hospital and tell them I'm coming."

I put our little boy inside my coat to keep him warm. With eyes blinded by tears, I screeched out of our driveway and sped to the hospital emergency room. "Please help me," I cried to a waiting nurse as I burst through the heavy double entrance doors to the hospital. Kind hands took Philip and rushed him to a nearby room. I knelt outside the emergency room door and prayed for God's mercy, not caring who saw me or what they might think.

After a while, an attending doctor came out of the room and walked over to me. He laid his hand upon my shoulder and shook his head. "He's gone. There was nothing we could do. We tried."

It was one of those sudden "crib deaths."

Joyce was standing in the doorway of our house when I returned alone. The look on my face told the story. Mother's Day had turned into a day of incredible grief and confusion for us. The tragedy was so sudden and so stark. We did the only thing we knew to do. We knelt and called out to the Lord for help.

Then we turned to the Word of God. I wasn't sure just where to begin reading. Instead, the Lord Himself led us to the message we so sorely needed:

> Grace be to you and peace from God our Father, and from the Lord Jesus Christ.
> Blessed be God, even the Father of our Lord Jesus Christ, the Father of mercies, and the God of all comfort;
> Who comforteth us in all our tribulation, that we may be able to comfort them which are in any trouble, by the comfort wherewith we ourselves are comforted of God (2 Corinthians 1:2-4, KJV).

I did not understand all that God was allowing to happen to us, but already He had made one thing abundantly clear. The Father of mercies was going to use our sorrow to make us a blessing to other people with broken hearts. He was going to heal us and then use our scars as a testimony.

Since that time, we have met so many who have suffered the heartache of losing a little one. I have watched others as they have tried to give comfort, and their words have seemed like scant drops of water on a blazing desert.

Then I have seen my wife put her arm around a brokenhearted mother and cry with her. I have seen my wife tell this distraught and brokenhearted mother that Jesus knows and cares and heals. Then I've seen that broken and

crushed life unfold and begin the road to healing and restored joy. *Only someone with scars can minister like that.*

If you're hurting, don't block out the pain with seda-
tives and lock out God. He loves you so much. And if He has
healed you, remember that *your scars may be your greatest
ministry!*

Roy
Rogers

Master of
My Fate

Roy and Dale Rogers were the most prominent of the famous Hollywood stars who joined with Dr. Henrietta Mears, Vonette, and me in starting the Hollywood Christian Group more than forty years ago. Spend time with Roy and you will sense as I have that you are speaking with a truly great man who possesses a genuine spirit of humility.

He grew up in a family in which music played an important role. He was strumming the guitar when he was eight and calling square dances at ten, meanwhile developing a fine singing voice and an unusual talent for yodeling.

Roy landed his first movie role in 1937 where he was cast as a singing cowboy. The King of Cowboys went on to star in eighty-seven musical westerns, becoming the number

*one box-office star in all westerns for twelve consecutive
years.*

*In 1947 Roy married Dale Evans, his leading lady in
thirty-five of his pictures. As one of America's most beloved
couples, they have endeared themselves to millions around the
world and experienced a full life of good times and tragic
experiences. Roy shares how God led him into his career and
how he has coped with times of trial through our Lord's
strength.*

Looking back over my life, I can see how the Lord has
had His hand on me for years, even when I made no effort to
know Him in a personal way.

When I was a boy, my family lived on a farm twelve
miles outside Portsmouth, Ohio. My mother was crippled
from polio, and my dad worked at a shoe factory in the
city—only coming home every other weekend. My three
sisters and I did all the farm chores. And because of the Great
Depression, we had very little money.

As a child I wanted to be a dentist, perhaps because
dental care was practically non-existent where we lived. If
you got a bad toothache, the tooth was pulled with hardly
any effective anesthetic.

But because of hard times, I had to drop that and
other dreams tied to a high school education and go to work
alongside Dad in the shoe factory in Cincinnati. Later, our
family visited my older sister in California and decided to
move there.

One day she talked me into playing guitar, singing
and yodeling in a local talent contest. I was shy, so she

literally had to push me on stage. I must have pleased some-body because I was asked to join a group which ultimately became "The Sons of the Pioneers." That was the start of my career in the entertainment business.

In those days I didn't go to church. I always believed in a power greater than myself, but knew nothing about a personal relationship with Jesus Christ. Yet God's hand guided me to the right places at the right times, and my career started to grow.

Republic Studios was looking for a new singing cow-boy. They had tested different fellows all morning when the vice president just "happened" to walk through the casting office and see me sitting there with my guitar and stetson. Immediately, he grabbed me and shoved me in front of the camera. I was on my way to stardom.

Five other singers auditioned at the same time. They were well-educated young men, not shy like me. And yet I was chosen. Why? I believe God had a work for me in family entertainment. He knew I was like "Popeye the Sailor Man" in the funny papers: "I yam what I yam and that's all I yam!" No facade, just me.

But first God had to change my heart, which wasn't until after I had met and married Dale Evans. It began one day when Dale shared a new excitement with me: "I've just made the greatest decision of my life. Today I dedicated my life to Jesus Christ. It's wonderful."

I was a skeptic about religion. But I smiled and lis-tened as she went on and on about the new feelings she was experiencing. When she had quieted, I said, "I'm glad for you if it makes you happy. But be careful. Just don't go over-board, okay?"

Dale didn't pressure me to accept her faith. Instead, she gathered the family in the evenings for Bible reading and prayer. She even bought me a new Bible. I could see the change in Dale but didn't understand her new joy.

Finally, one Saturday night I stood looking out our bedroom window after an incident at a party we had given that had strained our relationship. I thought about my responsibilities to my family, and it occurred to me that any financial provisions I might be able to leave for my children would someday be gone. The fame of being a movie star wouldn't last forever. I realized that I wanted my kids to remember me for something special, something that mattered. I wanted them to remember me as a daddy who took them to church on Sundays and helped them learn how to live a good Christian life.

The next morning as Dale was preparing to take the children to Sunday school and church, I came downstairs and informed her, "If you are going to church, I am going with you."

As we sat in the service, I bowed my head for a long time, thinking about the decision I should make. At the invitation I sat up and turned to Dale. "Mama, I'm going down there." I did go, accepting Jesus Christ as my Savior.

The next Sunday our oldest daughter, Cheryl, accepted Jesus. Both of us were baptized Palm Sunday evening. And a spiritual bond was formed in our family which has never been broken.

I am so grateful that Dale worked with God to bring me something I had longed for all my life—peace. Materially speaking, for years I had nothing. Then for years I had much. But I soon learned that having too much is worse than having too little. Nothing ever seemed quite right. I was restless, confused, unsatisfied. But in my walk with the Lord, I've learned that the power of prayer and the feeling of spiritual blessedness and the love of Jesus have no price tags.

Over the years, my trail has been a great one, sometimes bumpy, sometimes stormy, sometimes smooth and beautiful. But when I asked Jesus Christ to be my Savior and Lord in 1948, He took me at my word and has been working out His will for me ever since.

I do not have to understand all the sorrow Dale and I have suffered in the loss of three children, friends and parents. It is not for me to question, but to trust His overall plan for my life as the Bible teaches: "Trust in the Lord with all your heart, and lean not on your own understanding" (Proverbs 3:5, NKJ).

One of the tragedies we suffered was the death of our beautiful mongoloid daughter, Robin. For all her problems, her frailty and her handicaps, she was a happy, loving little girl who spread a warmth throughout our family that I will not even attempt to describe. Suffice it to say, Robin Elizabeth Rogers was someone special, and everyone in our home knew it. She was, as Dale has often said, more like an angel than a human being.

She brought a rare kind of peace to our home. I can remember so many evenings when I would come home from the studio, tired and not in the best mood, and go straight to see her. As I talked and played with her, everything would suddenly be okay.

Just before her second birthday, Robin went to be with the Lord. Making the funeral arrangements was one of the hardest things I've ever had to do. And as time passed, I became more and more aware of the magnificent things she had accomplished in her brief visit.

The deaths of our daughter Debbie and son Sandy were equally hard. But through these experiences, we learned to trust God in all our circumstances.

On the eve of my recent aorta surgery, my pastor prayed with me. When he finished, I told him, "I have had a long life and a good one. Whatever the Lord wants to do with me is all right."

God is a big, good God and makes no mistakes. I am grateful to Him for the blessings of my life, my country, my family, my career, and my many loyal friends. Even when I have stumbled and seemed to lose my way, He has come to my aid and brought my feet to a larger place of service. One of the greatest lessons I have learned in life is that He is the Master of my fate.

Robert H. Schuller

Tough People Last

What began as an outdoor church in a rented drive-in theater has fruitfully prospered into the 10,000-member Crystal Cathedral in Garden Grove, California, and the "Hour of Power" television ministry under its founding pastor, Dr. Robert Schuller.

Bob was actively involved in a Los Angeles Billy Graham Crusade when I first met him. He is a man with a great heart for God and a brilliant mind who has been called to communicate to nonbelievers in what he often refers to as "pre-evangelism." He knows the language of the marketplace and has the ear of multitudes who would not normally listen to religious messages.

In December 1989, Bob became the first non-Soviet

pastor ever to deliver a sermon on Soviet television, a message heard by an estimated two hundred million Soviet people.

He is the popular author of more than twenty-five books, including several which made the New York Times Best Seller list.

He learned his greatest lesson through the tragic motorcyle accident that injured his daughter Carol. Her positive spirit in the midst of her trial will touch your heart, just as it did his.

My daughter Carol lost her leg in a motorcycle accident in 1978. At the time, Mrs. Schuller and I were in Korea. On the long trip back to Iowa, I searched for the right thing to say. What would my first words to Carol be?

When we arrived at the hospital, I was shocked. Carol lay in her bed in intensive care, her body bruised, broken, and disfigured. But her spirits were whole and healthy. Immediately she solved the problem of what to say by speaking first: "I know why it happened, Dad. God wants to use me to help others who have been hurt."

It was this spirit that carried her through seven months of hospitalization, intravenous feedings, and consequent collapsed veins. This positive attitude gave her the courage to fight a raging infection that threatened her life and to hang on until a new drug was released by the FDA. (It was the right drug at the right time—a real miracle.)

It was that same positive attitude that helped Carol make the transition from hospital patient to a "handicapped" member of a family and school—and to feel normal and whole again.

The last picture we have of Carol with both legs is one taken when she was in her softball uniform. The athlete of the family, Carol loves to play softball.

The summer after her accident, she shocked me by saying, "Dad, I'm going to sign up for softball again this year."

"That's great," I responded, not wanting to discourage her.

At that time, Carol's artificial leg was attached just below the knee which was so stiff she could barely bend it at a thirty-degree angle. She walked very stiffly; running was out of the question.

However, I took her to the local school where all the parents were lining up with their daughters to register for the girls' softball team. Carol signed up and went to check out her uniform.

As she swung her stiff plastic leg into the car and rested her jersey, socks, and cap in her lap, I turned to her and said, "Carol, how do you expect to play ball if you can't run?"

With flashing eyes, she snapped back, "I've got that all figured out, Dad! When you hit home runs, you don't have to run."

My daughter is tough. She's a survivor. She hit enough home runs that season to justify her presence on the team!

Carol inspired everyone with her tenacity, too. She had six surgeries after that first amputation. Later, she took up skiing and won a gold medal in the qualifying races that admitted her to that elite corps of skiers participating in the National Ski Championships. In March 1983, she pulled her goggles on and took her place among the champions of her country—at the young age of eighteen!

Yes, she still walked with a limp. She drew curious looks from strangers. But her positive attitude and determination helped her even with that.

Several years ago, our family was privileged to be guests of the American-Hawaiian Steamship Company on a one-week cruise of the Hawaiian Islands. It was absolutely beautiful. During the trip, Carol was not in the least ashamed to be seen in shorts or swimming attire although her artificial leg covered her stump to just below the hip. But she was very conscious of the fact that people looked at her out of the corners of their eyes and wondered what had happened to her.

On this cruise, it was customary on the last night to have a talent show in which the passengers participated. Carol, then seventeen years old, surprised us by saying, "I'm going to be in the talent show tonight." Now Carol doesn't sing, and of course she doesn't dance. So, naturally, I was curious as to what she would do.

Friday night, my wife and I sat in the lounge along with six hundred other people. The stage was set in the big glorified cocktail lounge. As you can imagine, it was a very secular scene. The first acts performed were typical of amateur talent shows. Then it was Carol's turn.

She came on stage wearing neither shorts nor Hawaiian garb, but a full-length dress. She looked beautiful. Walking up to the microphone, she said, "I really don't know what talent is, but I thought this would be a good chance for me to give what I think I owe you all—an explanation. I know you've been looking at me all week, wondering about my fake leg. I thought I should tell you what happened.

"I was in a motorcycle accident. I almost died, but the doctors kept giving me blood, and my pulse came back. They amputed my leg below the knee, and later, they amputated through the knee. I spent seven months in the hospital—

202

seven months with intravenous antibiotics to fight infection."

She paused a moment, then continued. "If I've one talent, it's this: During that time, my faith became very real to me."

Suddenly a hush swept over the lounge. The waitresses stopped serving drinks. The glasses stopped clinking. Every eye was focused on this tall seventeen-year-old blonde.

She said, "I look at you girls who walk without a limp, and I wish I could walk that way. I can't, but this is what I've learned, and I want to leave it with you: It's not how you walk that counts, but who walks with you and with whom you walk."

Then she paused and said, "I'd like to sing a song about my friend, my Lord." And she sang.

> And He walks with me,
>   and He talks with me,
> And He tells me I am His own,
> And the joy we share
>   in our time of prayer (originally, "as we tarry there")
> None other has ever known. [1]

"Thank you." And she stepped down.

There was not a dry eye, not a life that wasn't touched that night.

By holding on, digging in, and making the most of what happened to her, Carol taught me one of the greatest lessons I've ever learned: Tough times never last, but tough people do.

When tough times come, we need to take tough action, to hold on until the tide turns for the better, to tenaciously dig in and bloom where we are planted, and to inspire people with our cheerful and positive attitude. In the

203

process, other people will be stimulated to choose noble and positive outlooks for their lives too.

William E. Simon

Joining the Fight

William E. Simon possesses one of the most brilliant financial minds in our country, demonstrated by his phenomenal success in the business world. He is chairman of the board of William E. Simon & Sons Inc., a company he founded in 1988. He has also served in many high-ranking posts in government and in the private sector.

A former president of the U.S. Olympic Committee, Bill currently chairs the U.S. Olympic Foundation and recently joined the board of directors of the World Cup '94 organizing committee.

Bill was appointed Deputy Secretary of the U.S. Treasury in 1973 and later that year became the first administrator of the Federal Energy office. In 1974 he was appointed Secretary of the Treasury and held that cabinet post for three years.

Even though Bill has a long list of accomplishments,

what impresses me even more is the earnest prayer from his sincere heart, "Lord, help me to know and obey Your will. I want to know Your plan for my life." His article shows how dramatically the Lord led through that prayer.

Suddenly a telephone call came that would change my life. It was from the White House. Out of the blue, I was being asked to fly immediately to Washington, D.C., to meet with newly re-elected President Nixon. The President, it seemed, was going to offer me a senior position in his administration.

The year was 1972. I was a senior partner at Salomon Brothers, one of the leading investment houses in New York. My wife Carol and I were blessed with seven beautiful children. And we had just built our dream house in New Vernon, New Jersey.

In short, we were a close and happy family, and we wanted for nothing. We had reached the point where we had always longed to be.

I remember putting down the phone and looking at Carol. She had exactly the same reactions that were tugging inside of me.

Certainly I felt pride, excitement and, above all, gratitude at the prospect of being asked to serve my country, especially during that critical time in our history. Divisive forces from the war in Vietnam and an increasingly unstable economy were tearing at the fabric of our country's freedom, prosperity and goodwill.

But I also felt some apprehension and foreboding. After all, why should I interrupt a successful career and uproot my family to venture into that political snake pit in Washington?

I vastly preferred the free-wheeling, rough-and-tumble of the business world to the encrusted and too often cryptic cocoon of bureaucratic life in government. What's more, the contrast between modern-day Washington and the city built as a proud trademark to the ideals of the Founding Fathers filled me with sorrow.

In my view, Washington had become an elitist, self-absorbed city that cared little for the values of everyday Americans who believe deeply in the work ethic and in family, freedom and faith in God. And behind those majestic monuments in the back rooms of Congress, I knew that self-serving politicians were busily spending and borrowing America ever deeper into debt.

Yet in the end, all of those reservations only reinforced the consideration Carol and I came to see as critical: If you truly fear for your country and if you fear for freedom, then how can you stand by and see the battle lost without joining the fight?

I knew that I couldn't stand by. I had to join the fray. And I also believed fervently that when your President asks you to serve, it is your duty to do so.

So I did. I met with President Nixon and gratefully accepted his offer. In early 1973, our family packed our bags, said goodbye to New Jersey, and headed south to a new adventure.

And what an adventure it was!

Little did I realize that when I accepted the President's offer, I would land in the eye of two economic cyclones that swept over the country during my years in office.

I was the "energy czar" during the OPEC oil embargo which sent prices soaring at the gas pumps. For the first time,

Americans realized that they had lost their energy independence.

And I was treasury secretary under President Ford during the worst peacetime inflation and recession to rock the country in forty years.

Not a bad political baptism! I worked eighteen-hour days, devoured thousands of briefing papers, appeared before more than three hundred congressional committees, and learned more about energy and the economy in my first four months on the job than I had during four years in college.

I was determined to do everything humanly possible to break the insane cycle of boom and bust that had begun with the decade that encompassed the Great Society and led to steadily worsening inflation, recession, economic dislocations and instability. Our mission was to get America off that disastrous economic roller coaster.

Although we worked as a team, I came to appreciate that true leadership is lonely. Certainly it was lonely for great men like Washington, Lincoln and Eisenhower.

And it was lonely for President Ford as well. Especially when he vetoed sixty-six bills in two years—and made fifty-four vetoes stick—in his unflinching quest to break the back of big government accompanied by out-of-control spending.

The media ridiculed us. Our opponents demagogued us.

There were days when my secret thoughts drifted back to our quiet and happy times in New Jersey. But, in retrospect, I would never trade that experience in Washington for all the material comforts and security in the world because, as our country pulled together and we overcame the aftermath of Vietnam and the tragedy of Watergate, the Ford Administration ended in January 1977 with America's spirits uplifted and our nation back on track. Inflation was down dramatically, our economy was growing again with renewed vigor, and through it all, the principles of freedom—and the inextricable link between personal, political and economic freedom—were raised up and reaffirmed.

This gave me a tremendous feeling of satisfaction. I had responded to my country's call and served America in her hour of need.

So, for me, the greatest lesson will always be that alongside one's devotion to family, there is no higher duty, nor greater honor, than serving your country—not just in a governmental position, but also in our military, in our communities and our neighborhoods.

Life is not a dress rehearsal, and rarely are we given the opportunity to do something twice. I'm not sure where my life would have led had I declined the President's request and stayed on the well-travelled road I was following on Wall Street. But by listening to my instincts, taking a risk, and beginning a new journey on an unknown road, I learned more about life, discovered more about myself, stretched my horizons farther, and savored experiences far richer than I would otherwise have ever known.

Some people might call it fate. Some might call it luck. But some of us would call it God's plan.

Kenneth Taylor

Two Life-Changing Events

Daily my life is enriched because of the creative, brilliant mind and dedicated heart of Dr. Kenneth Taylor, translator of the Living Bible. Though I possess and study God's Word from many translations, my favorite is this culturally relevant paraphrase which God has used in the lives of tens of millions around the world.

Dr. Taylor is a noted scholar, author and publisher. Currently he serves as chairman of the board of Tyndale House Publishers and as international chairman emeritus of Living Bibles International. He is also a member of the advisory board for the Christian Embassy, a ministry of Campus Crusade for Christ.

Kenneth is the author of many books including My

First Bible In Pictures, *which won an Angel Award in 1990. He has also been inducted into the Christian Booksellers Association Hall of Fame.*

Kenneth tells about two turning points in his life, one when he was a young man and the other when he was older. Both demonstrate his openness to the Lord's leading that I have observed in his life.

Instead of one lesson, I'm going to relate two. One took place during college days, and the other when I was forty-five years old.

During college vacations, I worked in the hay fields near Portland, Oregon, my childhood home. But Sunday work was not allowed in our family, so on a certain Sunday afternoon, while the baling crew was sweating through the hot, ten-hour day, I went to church. After our family dinner, I picked up a book from my father's library and spent the afternoon reading it.

The book looked interesting, for it was a biography of another college student, Bill Borden of Yale University, class of 1909. I became fascinated as I read because he had such a love for God and for his fellow human beings. Those were qualities I longed to have in my own life. I was eager to see how he got that way so I could follow his example.

Bill Borden came from a wealthy home. His father had left him a million dollars—currently worth at least ten times that much. But Bill didn't try to keep his inheritance because he had given himself to God, and he felt that everything he had was a trust from God. So he gave away hundreds of thousands of dollars.

I was aghast. Since childhood I had thought becoming a millionaire one of life's highest goals, even though in my case it was impossible to reach.

But here was Bill Borden, a college senior, giving great riches away. He was a spiritual giant in other ways, too. He frequently talked with his classmates about God—that He had a plan for their lives, including the forgiveness of their sins through faith in Jesus Christ. At that time, I don't think I had ever talked with an unbeliever about Christ, and the thought terrified me. Perhaps this was a reaction to my father's almost-embarrassing readiness to tell others about the Savior. Yet here was my hero, Bill Borden, starting a gospel mission to preach to poor street people. He would go there on Saturday nights and put his arm around men who came forward, telling them about Christ's willingness to forgive and help them.

I also admired Bill's experience on the Yale wrestling team; he knew some of the agonies I had experienced when pinned to the mat.

But as I read further about this millionaire, athlete, and spiritual giant, I became uneasy. He was thinking of becoming a missionary! Now that was something I knew I would never be—not because I had prayed and decided on the basis of God's will, but because I just didn't want to go. I didn't want to give up the good things of life in America, and I didn't want Bill Borden to do it either!

But he did just that. After Yale University he attended Princeton Seminary and became greatly concerned about Chinese Muslims, for whom it seemed little was being done by mission societies. After being ordained in Moody Church, his home church in Chicago, he applied to and was accepted by the China Inland Mission. The mission board assigned him to a western province in China heavily populated by Muslims. In preparation, he went to Egypt to study the Arabic language and Muslim literature.

212

As I read, I became increasingly uncomfortable. Suppose God called *me* to be a missionary. Would I go? I wasn't willing to face the question and tried to put it out of my mind.

Then I read that Bill became ill after only a few weeks in Egypt. But I had read missionary stories before, and I knew of wonderful miracles of healing because people trusted in God. Well, I was entirely unprepared as I turned the page to find that Bill's fever grew higher and higher. "Dear God," I prayed as I followed the story, "*don't* let him die."

But he did die. God let Bill Borden die. I was overwhelmed by shock. Then a cold, hard resolution gripped me. "If that is the way God treats a man wholly devoted to Him, then I want no more of such a God." It was a terrible moment as I deliberately turned my back on God. It was as if I were stepping off a cliff and plunging to the rocks below.

But God was gracious beyond expression. He reached out and grabbed me and pulled me back. I can't explain what happened—apart from God—but suddenly I found myself on my knees beside the chair where I had been sitting. I was praying in deep contrition, "Lord, here is my life. Take it and use it in any way You want to."

I have never turned back from that decision—a decision that completely changed my direction in life. It was a decision that made it possible for God to lead me on a guided tour for the rest of my life.

I also experienced another life-changing event. Many, many years later as an adult, I attended a Campus Crusade seminar for business people. When I arrived, I found out to my horror that part of the program was to leave the conference grounds and tell someone the Good News concerning Christ dying for our sins and redeeming us for heaven. I literally clenched my teeth to make myself carry out the assignment. I started out across a nearby park to find someone I could talk to, hoping against hope that no one would be there! But of course, there was! A young black man was sitting against a tree. I sat down beside him and tried to open a conversation with a few pleasantries about the weather. But he didn't seem to notice me and had little responsiveness to my overtures. Finally I took courage and asked him if he ever read the Bible.

He said no.

So I told him about some things in Scripture, especially about its promises to those who believe. The young man was somewhat interested but not to the point of making a life-changing decision.

I left him with mingled emotions: sadness because of his little chance for happiness, hope that the tiny seed I had planted would grow, and elation that I had carried out a hard task. But that experience was, in fact, a turning point in my life. I had discovered that telling a stranger about our Lord was not an impossible thing for me to do, and after that it became simpler to witness to others about God's love—though not easy.

John F.
Walvoord

God Is Faithful

*Dr. John F. Walvoord is the chancellor of Dallas
Theological Seminary where he served as president for thir-
ty-four years. He impressed me many years ago with his
brilliant theological mind and burning heart for Christ.*

*Through the years he has helped to give a strong
emphasis to the authority and inerrancy of God's holy, inspired Word, for which I am personally indebted, as is the
whole Body of Christ.*

Dr. Walvoord is the author of many books, including
The Prophecy Knowledge Handbook, What We
Believe: Discovering the Truths of Scripture *and his
current bestseller,* Armageddon, Oil and the Middle East
Crisis. *He also served as co-editor for the Old and New
Testament editions of* The Bible Knowledge Commen-
tary *and is a member of the revision committee for the New
Scofield Reference Edition of the Holy Bible.*

215

THE GREATEST LESSON...

Throughout his lifetime, Dr. Walvoord has experienced the touch of God on his work and in his family life. He shares how God has led him into exciting ministry opportunities and faith-stretching circumstances, including the accidental death of one of his sons.

God's faithfulness for me started early—even before I was born. My mother had been chronically ill, and the doctor advised an abortion to preserve her health as well as to avoid an abnormal baby. As a committed Christian, however, she would have nothing to do with this suggestion. Her prayers were answered when I was born a perfectly normal child. Indeed, her own health improved, and she lived almost to the age of 102.

After several years of catechism, I joined the church at age 9. When I was 12 years old, I decided to be a minister of the gospel. But at age 15 catastrophe struck. My father suddenly lost his job as superintendent of schools in our town because he had forbidden the sale of beer at the high school dances. His stand was too much for the German community in which we lived. The beer interests raised a political fund and elected a board of education that fired him. It seemed like the end of the world to us at the time. But, in fact, this incident led to an event that would transform my life.

We moved to Racine, Wisconsin, where my father had found new employment. That first fall I joined a Bible class taught by Dr. William McCarrell of the Cicero Bible Church. The class was held in the Sixth Avenue Methodist Church which was rented for the occasion. On the second night, as he was teaching Galatians, Dr. McCarrell said, "You can't be good enough to be saved." These words hit me like a lightning bolt. After all, I wasn't bad; I did the best I could. Wasn't that enough? He then explained that Christ had to die for our sins. Immediately I accepted this truth. The next morning I realized something had happened to me. I had been spiritually born again.

Upon graduating from high school I had to decide which college I would attend. My brother and sister had gone to a denominational school which was at least nominally religious. But some of my friends were going to Wheaton College, a small, struggling school which had just been accredited. I went to Wheaton. The first Sunday night after my arrival, Percy Crawford, an upperclassman, led an evangelistic meeting and gave an appeal for complete surrender to Christ. Determined to make the will of God the rule of my life, I went forward. The commitment I made that night has never wavered.

Upon my graduation from Wheaton, the choice of seminary was before me. In the East a prestigious seminary with a long history, large faculty, and a great reputation was open, but I had heard about a new school in Dallas, later to be called Dallas Theological Seminary. It was obviously evangelical and had sixty-five students and only a few faculty members, none of them with earned doctor's degrees. In my confusion I went to Dr. J. Oliver Buswell, president of Wheaton College, for guidance. He listened to my story and said quietly, "I think you'll get a good education at Dallas." This settled the matter for me.

My experience at Dallas was a happy one. More than a fourth of the entering class of twenty-five had been fellow classmates at Wheaton. But upon approaching seminary graduation, I faced the necessity of applying to a mission board.

I had long believed that I was called to be a missionary in China, so I sent a letter asking for an application form

217

to the China Inland Mission. When the application arrived, I spread it on my bed, got down on my knees, and asked the Lord for guidance. He very definitely said I should not send it in. Thinking I had chosen the wrong country, I asked for an application for India from another mission board. God again said no. Apparently, for reasons beyond my understanding, He did not want me on the mission field.

As a result, I remained at Dallas and enrolled in the doctoral program. As I neared the completion of this degree, I began to look for a pastoral position. In the first church in which I candidated, I discovered that the world was not waiting for me even though I was a Dallas graduate. The congregation showed no interest whatsoever.

The next church was located in the midst of a booming oil field and was the only church permitted within a ten-mile radius. The area had a population of 8,000 people. I spoke to crowded meetings Sunday morning and Sunday night and was asked to become the pastor. This was it—a mission field right in my own country. But the Lord said no. It seemed to me that I would not have a better opportunity to minister as a pastor than what was just offered to me. What was I to do?

I recalled that the year before, I had been offered the job as registrar at Dallas Seminary but had no interest in it. I told the Lord that if He wanted me to take this position, President Lewis Sperry Chafer would have to renew the invitation. Within ten days President Chafer called me into his office. This time he offered not only the registrar's position, which was really heading up all the educational programs of the seminary, but also half of the theology department which he taught. During our meeting, he solemnly set me apart in prayer for what proved to be fifty years of faculty service, the last thirty-three years as president.

On my departure that day, he announced that I

would receive a salary of $100 per month. But I didn't pay any attention to his words because I knew the seminary could not afford it. Six months later my salary was raised, but I didn't know about it for three years. What I have learned in life, however, is that God is faithful. I never had a financial obligation I could not pay and never suffered a lack of anything that I really needed.

Three years after I began on the seminary's faculty, I married a wonderful helpmate, Geraldine, for whom I have been daily grateful ever since. Our first son John was born three years later and proved to be an unusually precocious and bright child. Later, he earned a Th.D. from Dallas Theological Seminary and a Ph.D. from Columbia University.

Our second son James was born three years after John. He was slightly handicapped, both mentally and physically, and was not able to walk until two years of age. We placed him in special schools from the time he was three, but he has never been able to function completely on his own and presently is living at the Marbridge Ranch near Austin, Texas, with about a hundred other men who are also slightly handicapped. He is a knowledgeable Christian with an outgoing personality who thoroughly enjoys life.

Our third son Timothy was born some years later. He turned out to have unusual ability. In his large high school, he was chosen to be one of thirty honor students given special privileges in choosing the courses they wanted. Moving on to Wheaton College, he completed the four-year course in two years and nine months and graduated in the top two percent of his class. Consequently he had no difficulty getting into the medical school he wanted in Texas. After his first year, he married Dawn, a college classmate. Upon graduating from medical school, he immediately took his state board exams and passed them with flying colors.

During his senior year in medical school Timothy

taught a high school Bible class and a college-age Bible class at a little Baptist church near the school. Because of the church's regard for Timothy, they gave a special send-off service one Sunday. The following Sunday they held a memorial service for him—he had been instantly killed by a large truck which had moved suddenly into his path on an interstate highway.

One may ask, "Why?" Of the thousand letters we received from sympathetic friends, Dr. W. A. Criswell's expressed it simply: "Some Christians get ready for heaven sooner than others."

Our fourth child, Paul, was hopelessly retarded, mentally and physically, and has spent most of his years in a state school where he will stay for the rest of his life.

What is the greatest lesson I've learned? That God sustains us. In times of triumph, in times of sorrow, in times of achievement, in times of disappointment—our God is faithful.

Pat
Williams

The Secret to Success
in the Marketplace

Pat Williams became a part of our lives more than twenty years ago when one of our staff introduced him to Christ through the Four Spiritual Laws gospel presentation. Over the years, our paths have crossed and with each meeting, our hearts have been drawn closer together. More recently, Pat has played a significant role as chairman of the fundraising committee in helping Campus Crusade for Christ relocate its international headquarters from San Bernardino, California, to Orlando, Florida.

Pat is president and general manager of the Orlando Magic, the National Basketball Association (NBA) franchise in Orlando. He is widely recognized throughout the sports world as a consummate promoter and astute talent scout.

THE GREATEST LESSON...

While he enjoys a widespread reputation in worldwide sporting circles, many consider him to be one of this country's premier motivational and humorous speakers. He is the author of a number of motivational books offering inspiration and wit, among which are Making Magic, The Power Within You, Rekindled *and* Love Her . . . Like Him.

From his years as a successful businessman, Pat has learned many lessons about conducting himself in a godly manner. Here he gives us the rules he goes by to pattern his life after biblical principles.

For men, all too often the biggest three-letter word in our language is *ego*.

Have you ever noticed that the first thing we ask a man we meet is not, "How are you as a father?" or "What kind of husband are you?" but rather, "What do you do?"

Particularly with a man, too often the job becomes the number one priority. I'm convinced our ego drives make this so. We feel that if we are not succeeding in our work, we're not succeeding at all.

But everything goes out of whack when that happens, so it's worth a daily struggle, if necessary, to keep the priorities in order.

This doesn't mean that during the time you're being paid, you're giving less than total effort. Your paycheck is housing you, clothing you, feeding your family. You owe your employer a great deal for that.

The greatest trade for your paycheck is yourself. Your character is a gift to your boss. It makes you what you are, determines whether you'll be a success, and charts how valuable you are to the company.

When I was in Spartanburg, South Carolina, with the Phillies organization, one of the owners of the ball club was Mr. R. E. Littlejohn. He was a committed Christian. He knew the Lord, loved and served Him and believed that God, not man, has control in the affairs of men. He believed that our sovereign God has a plan for the world, and that He is ordering history according to that plan. He made a tremendous impact on me and from him I learned some of my greatest lessons in life.

What made him so special? Christlikeness. That's not an attribute anyone should throw around lightly. And I don't. I realize what I'm saying when I say a human being is like Christ. It's the highest compliment that can be paid. The way Mr. Littlejohn conducted himself in his personal life and his business affairs made me want to emulate him.

Over dinner one day, I reminded Mr. Littlejohn of the many things I'd learned from him and suggested we try to get his principles down on paper. A couple of hours of brainstorming produced what I like to call The Littlejohn Rules for Success in the Marketplace. You'll find that they're based on reverse-style, paradoxical living. I trust that his advice will be as valuable to you as it is to me.

The Littlejohn Rules for Success in the Marketplace

1. *Have faith in God, and seek divine guidance in every decision, no matter how big or small.*

2. *Sell yourself to others. They must have confidence in you so they can depend on you, trust you, believe you, and confide in you. You only get one chance to make a good first impression.*

223

3. *Never give the other fellow the impression that you think you know more than he does. If you do, you will break his spirit and destroy your influence with him, losing your ability to communicate properly.*

4. *Seek information from other people who are more experienced and be willing to listen to their advice. Be humble and willing to learn from anyone—regardless of his station in life. One good way to measure a person's character is to observe the way he treats people who can't possibly do him any good.*

5. *Work hard. Put first things first. Work as if you would live forever; live as if you would die tomorrow. Be willing to sacrifice some pleasures in order to do what has to be done.*

6. *Remember that everything you do in life leaves an impression on somebody. You are being observed every minute of each day, and every move is being recorded in someone's mind, either as a plus or a minus.*

7. *Don't expect everyone to agree with your ideas, but if the majority of people disagree on a subject, it's wise to make a new appraisal of your position.*

8. *It is necessary to control the things you have control over, no matter how small they may seem.*

9. *If you don't have a good feeling about a decision, don't make it. Never make an important decision without sleeping on it for two nights.*

10. *Don't make things complicated. Most good things in life are simple and practical.*

11. *Learn to manage your own personal affairs before expecting anyone to trust you with operating the affairs of their business.*

12. *To build loyalty and cooperation, take a personal interest in the feelings and welfare of other people you are working with.*

13. *Don't run from problems. A real problem gives you an opportunity to sell yourself to others. It's not the problem that matters so much, but how you react to it. The gem cannot be polished without friction, nor the child of God cleansed without adversity.*

14. *Surround yourself with successful people. The greatness of a man shows when he is able to see the greatness in others.*

15. *Be a good listener. Ask questions and get the other fellow to express his opinion first.*

16. *Gain experience. Pay your dues. You can't start at the top. You must learn at all levels to become an effective executive.*

Mr. Littlejohn patterned his life after these biblical principles. Some might say that his are the rules of a weak, nonassertive type. They're wrong. He was a successful businessman, a successful baseball club owner, a successful husband and father, a successful employer. And he was also a successful, witnessing Christian.

The best advice from such an outstanding example of a Christian? He would say not to look at him. Look to Christ, the author of unconditional love who said, "Greater love hath no man than this, that a man lay down his life for his friends" (John 15:13, KJV). *That*, Mr. Littlejohn would tell you, is the example we should follow.

Ralph D. Winter

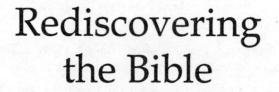

Rediscovering the Bible

Highly regarded as a missions scholar, Dr. Ralph D. Winter is the founder and director of the United States Center for World Mission (USCWM). Its purpose is to help existing missions agencies focus their own strategies and mobilization efforts to reach the "hidden peoples"—those populations where no indigenous church exists.

My friendship with Ralph goes back to the days when we were students together at Princeton and later at Fuller Theological Seminary. He has always stood out among the crowd with his vision, creative ideas and dedication to helping fulfill the Great Commission. His concern for the world caused him to launch a prayer campaign called Frontier Fellowship which seeks to involve a million people in praying for the 12,000 unreached people groups of the world.

RALPH D. WINTER

In this account, Ralph provides thought-provoking insights into the historical significance of the Bible.

A few years ago I learned an amazing lesson I often refer to as "the greatest intellectual revolution in my life." It took me completely by surprise. The lesson did not even soak in fully for a number of months. But it catapulted me into extraordinary consternation and anxious research.

For years, I had known about certain passages in the Old Testament which echoed in advance the Great Commission of our Lord recorded in Matthew 28:18-20; namely, sharing the knowledge of God with all the nations and tribes and tongues of the earth. This idea is found in the Old Testament in a number of places.

But somehow I had gotten the basic impression that the Old Testament was "outmoded" by the New Testament. For example, people didn't exactly get "born again" in the Old Testament. They did not go around witnessing for Christ. Nor did they form mission societies to send people to the ends of the earth. The people of God of the Old Testament mainly struggled with their own personal, family and national problems.

Up to this time, I had heard many different views of the Bible's significance:

1. *The Medicine Chest Bible:* Early as a Christian, I thought of the Old Testament and the Bible in general as something like a medicine chest—where you look when something goes wrong. If your marriage is in trouble, see page xxx. If you have aches and pains, see pages xxx. That's why it made sense to put all those suggestions in the front of Gideon Bibles placed in hotels.

2. *The Snack Bar Bible:* Later, I began to discover all the good, positive, and inspiring things in the Bible. Sunday school teachers hauled out this verse. The pastor's sermon highlighted that one. Great stuff. Like reaching into a well-stocked refrigerator—good things on every shelf.

3. *The Crystal Ball Bible:* Pretty soon, most of the really good verses became well known to me. But there still remained the possibility of getting fascinated by biblical prophecy. For some people that is the ultimate in the Bible. They ransack every reference to the future to find out what is going to happen.

But in all of this, the Old Testament was not a whole lot more than a source book: a grab-bag of stories for children and a book of sermon illustrations for adults.

However, that first 75 percent of the Bible, the Old Testament, did tell the continuous story of a nation. I finally got Israel's history straight in my mind:

- Abraham coming over from Kuwait to Israel
- his descendants getting carried off to Egypt for four hundred years
- Moses bringing the survivors back to Palestine, with a big interlude in the desert
- the rocky period of the Judges, the Kings, and the two kingdoms
- the dispersion of the northern group
- the exile of the Judean group
- the trickling back of these Judeans (Jews) under Ezra and Nehemiah
- the Greek and Roman domination of the politics and culture of the hardy survivors.

228

And finally the bright, blue yonder opens up and God strategically intervenes in human history as Jesus, His only Son, appears among men.

Wow! This is so important. Why bother about all that detailed background? Isn't that for seminary students? Or for sermonizers to mine for practical applications and illustrations for their messages? How important is the Old Testament if the New Testament is so *new*?

Actually, the terms *Old* and *New*, as handy and familiar as they are, don't tell the full story. The New Testament, in an important sense, begins with Genesis 12! Abraham was the first Gentile proselyte, the beginning of God's outreach to the whole world.

The Old Testament is thus not just the description of what preceded Jesus' arrival. From Abraham on, the major portion of the Bible is the story of what happened in an unfolding plan that has, from 2000 B.C. until now, been the single major event of relentless missionary outreach to the nationalities, tribes and tongues of the world.

Every commentator on Genesis breaks the book at Genesis chapter 12. In fact, a Bible could be published in which Genesis 1-11 would be called the Introduction; Genesis 12-50 labeled chapter 1; Exodus, chapter 2; Leviticus, chapter three, and so on. The title of this new edition could be *The Kingdom Strikes Back*.

For example, Genesis 1-11 portrays (1) the goodness of God's creation, (2) the gruesome entrance of evil, and (3) the hopelessness of the result—"every intent of [man's] heart was doing evil continually" (Genesis 6:5, NKJ). What an introduction!

But what is next? What does God do now?

Well, Genesis 12 (the beginning of our new chapter 1) opens with—and initiates—the astounding plan where God chooses one man and one nation through whom He can reclaim all mankind. The Lord informs Abraham that He has decided to make him a child of God by faith—right then and there! "I will bless you" in verse 2 means adoption, including all of the New Testament concept of reconciliation. Jesus reaffirmed this when He said, "Abraham rejoiced to see My day, and he saw it and was glad" (John 8:56, NKJ). Abraham's sins were covered by the blood of Christ.

God also tells Abraham that not only his own lineage, but all of the peoples of the earth, will also be blessed (adopted)—beginning right then and there! The Book of Revelation assures us that some from every tribe and tongue and nation will participate in this adoptive reconciliation (Revelation 5:9).

Okay, Okay, Okay, why is this so significantly different? Why did this mean so much to me? Because the great bulk of the Bible is no longer an up-and-down story of what happened before the sparks began to fly, before God's major plan began to move forward. *It is the story of a nation that received a commission and did not fully live up to it.*

Note well: If one nation received the blessing of heavenly inheritance and could and should pass it on to all other peoples, how did this chosen nation do? The Old Testament tells us the gripping story of Israel *under orders,* a commission it partially carried out and then handed on to other nations.

Now, all of a sudden, I understand why God moved Abraham and his family from Kuwait to Israel: because that was the land-bridge connecting Europe and Asia and Africa—a better place from which to reach out to the whole world.

Now I see God gently pushing this budding nation into Egypt *as a missionary operation.*

Now I understand that the Mosaic Exodus brought God's people out of Egypt *so they could reach out to all the*

230

peoples of the earth—even though their self-centered struggles blinded them to this continuing obligation and privilege. (Check Jonah's inability to get it straight.)

Now I view the "dispersion" of the northern group as not just a punishment, but as part of *God's missionary concern to reach out to other nations.* The same goes for the Judean exile: the Jews' longing to return to their land clashed with God's purposes for sending them—"You should be My salvation *to the ends of the earth!"* (Isaiah 49:6, NKJ)

Now I also understand Jesus' anger at the money-changers who took up the space intended as *the court of the Gentiles* in "a house of prayer for all nations" (Matthew 21:12; Isaiah 56:7, NKJ).

But a new thought really clinched the matter for me. The absence of evidence that Abraham's descendants took the Great Commission seriously prior to the appearance of the Christ is no more proof that the clear commission in Genesis 12:2,3 was not yet in force than would it be proof that the New Testament repetition of the Great Commission was not yet in force just because the vast majority of God's New Testament peoples paid virtually no attention to it in the eighteen centuries following the New Testament!

Where is the Great Commission in Chrysostom's sermons, or Tertullian's, or Augustine's? Or where is it to be seen in the Nicean Creed, the Chalcedonian creed, the Augsburg (Lutheran) Confession, or the Westminster Confession? *Its absence does not prove Jesus intended it for later attention* in modern times—by, say, William Carey.

Suddenly I saw the history of the United States, the history of Russia, and recently the history of Korea—and of every other nation that has heard the gospel—as stories of nations under this commission. That is, the Old Testament experience is a dynamic, full blown *parallel* (not a preface) to

231

our own national experience and to other similarly "blessed" nations.

But now that our people (of the United States) have received that same blessing, how are we doing? Is our nation foggy on this point? Do the 137 languages spoken in Los Angeles have a clear missionary significance to Americans, or even American evangelicals? Are we unaware that God is a missionary God from start to finish?

Now I understood completely. Instead of being the story of a nation not yet commissioned but merely exhorted to "behave," the Bible is a new, exciting book, full of insights, missionary strategy, and up-to-date applications of how God wants to teach and use His people to finish the Great Commission.

For me, this is the greatest lesson I have ever learned.

Bill Bright

───◆───

How to Love the Unloveable

Like the rest of the authors of this book, I have made many important discoveries and learned many valuable lessons in the course of my seventy years.

I could have written of my days of agnosticism when as a happy pagan I finally heard the Good News for the first time and fell in love with Jesus Christ.

I could have told about the days when I first experienced the reality of the person and ministry of the Holy Spirit.

I could have shared my discovery of how to introduce others to Christ as a way of life, or my realization that everybody hungers for God, even the so-called atheists, because God created us that way (Romans 1:19,20).

However, having considered all of these possibilities, I have chosen to write about how I learned to love people who sometimes are difficult to love.

Why was this lesson important to me? Because God places a very strong emphasis on love in His Word. In fact, our Lord teaches us to "love the Lord your God with all your heart, soul, and mind" and to "love your neighbor as much as you love yourself. All other commandments and all the demands of the prophets stem from these two laws and are fulfilled if you obey them" (Matthew 22:37-40, TLB).

Jesus reminds us in John 13:35, "By this all men will know that you are my disciples, if you love one another" (NIV).

And again, the Holy Spirit spoke through the apostle Paul, as he records in 1 Corinthians 13, that no matter what else we might accomplish in life, regardless of what we may contribute that is good and commendable, apart from love it is of no value whatever.

Further, I was sobered by the message which God sent to the church at Ephesus. This church was mightily used by God to touch the wicked city of Ephesus. However, approximately thirty years after the apostle Paul was martyred for his Christian faith the church had left its first love. God threatened to remove their candlestick from its place among the churches unless they repented and returned to that first love (Revelation 2:1-7).

With such emphasis in God's Word on loving Christ and one another, I finally concluded that the most important contribution I can make to this book is the revolutionary discovery I made many years ago on how to love by faith.

Is there someone in your life whom you have difficulty loving? Have you ever experienced a conflict with another person that left you with bitter or angry feelings?

There was a period in my ministry when I was faced with such a challenge. Several men in whom I had placed great confidence, who were in positions of leadership in Campus Crusade for Christ, were unfaithful to that trust. This resulted in misunderstandings all across the nation of what our ministry was about. The situation was fraught with tremendous crises and had a potential for anger, resentment, discord and conflict. A godly resolution required a full measure of my love for these men.

For years I had spoken on the subject of love. I had a simple four-point outline:

1. God loves you unconditionally.

2. You are commanded to love others—God, your neighbors, your enemies.

3. You are incapable of loving others in your own strength.

4. You can love others with God's love.

But, as in the case of most sermons on love, something was missing. I still did not grasp one essential ingredient for enabling God to love through me—despite the circumstances.

One night at the beginning of this crisis, I was awakened at 2 A.M. I knew that God had something to say to me. I felt impressed to get out of bed, take my Bible and go into another room so I wouldn't disturb my wife, Vonette. I fell to my knees and read and prayed for the next couple of hours.

What I discovered that night has since enriched my life and the lives of tens of thousands of others. I had never heard anyone speak on the lesson God revealed to me. Yet it was so simple, so biblical and so revolutionary. The discovery? *Christians can love by faith.*

As a result of applying this lesson, the situation that had such a vast potential for destruction was resolved. And God never allowed me to have any resentment or antagonism toward my brothers. In fact, I continue to love them to this day.

Truly, love is the greatest privilege and power known to man. When Christ came into my life and I became a Christian, God gave me the resources to be a different person. He gave me the ability to love. But I did not discover how to make that love a practical reality in my life until that night on my knees.

Everything in the Christian life, I knew, was based on faith. God's holy Word says, *"Without faith* it is impossible to please Him"* (Hebrews 11:6, NASB). "The just shall live *by faith"* (Romans 1:17, NKJ) and "everything that does not come from *faith* is sin" (Romans 14:23, NIV). Then, that memorable night, God showed me that we love by faith just as we received Christ by faith, just as we are filled with the Holy Spirit by faith, and just as we walk in the Spirit by faith. Likewise, there can be no demonstration of God's love apart from faith.

It is God's will for us to love. Jesus *commands,* "Love each other as much as I love you" (John 15:12, TLB). He would not command us to do anything that He will not enable us to do if only we trust and obey Him. In 1 John 5:14,15, God *promises,* "If we ask anything according to his will, he hears us. And if we know that he hears us—whatever we ask—we know that we have what we asked of him" (NIV). Relating this *promise* to God's *command* to love, I discovered: *We can claim by faith the privilege of loving with His love.* In order to experience and share this love, we must claim it by faith; that is, trust His promise that He will give us all that we need to do His will on the basis of His *command* and *promise.*

Love is an act of the will and not of our emotions. Because we are obeying a command of God, we are not being hypocritical when we say, "I love you," even though we may not feel loving.

This truth is not new. It has been recorded in God's Word for two thousand years. But it was a revolutionary discovery to me that early morning some years ago and, since that time, to many thousands of other Christians with whom I have shared it. When I began to practice loving others by faith, I found that problems of tension with other individuals seemed to disappear, often miraculously.

In one instance, I was having difficulty loving a fellow staff member. This troubled me. I wanted to love him. I knew that God's Word commanded me to love him; yet, because of certain areas of inconsistency and personality differences, I found it difficult to love him. But the Lord reminded me of 1 Peter 5:7, "Let him have all your worries and cares, for he is always thinking about you and watching everything that concerns you" (TLB). I decided to give this problem to Him and love this man *by faith.* When I claimed God's love for the man by faith, my concern lifted. I knew the matter was in God's hands.

An hour later, I found a letter under my door from that very man, who had no possible way of knowing what I had just experienced. In fact, his letter had been written the day before. The Lord had foreseen the change in me. This friend and I met that afternoon and had the most wonderful time of prayer and fellowship we had ever experienced together. Loving with God's love by faith had changed our relationship.

I have seen this principle at work in many situations since then. For example, two gifted attorneys had great professional animosity, even hatred for each other. Even though they were distinguished members of the same firm, they were constantly criticizing and making the other's life miserable.

One of the men received Christ through our ministry and some months later came to me for counsel.

"I have hated and criticized my partner for years," he said, "and he has been equally antagonistic toward me. But now that I am a Christian, I don't feel right about continuing our warfare. What shall I do?"

"Why not ask your partner to forgive you and tell him that you love him?" I suggested.

"I could never do that!" he exclaimed. "That would be hypocritical. I *don't* love him. How could I tell him I love him when I don't?"

I explained the greatest lesson I had ever learned: that God commands His children to love even their enemies and that His supernatural, unconditional love is an expression of our will, not our emotions, which we exercise by faith.

Together we knelt to pray, and my friend asked God's forgiveness for his critical attitude toward his law partner and claimed God's love for him by faith.

Early the next morning, my friend walked into his partner's office and announced, "Something wonderful has happened to me. I have become a Christian. And I have come to ask you to forgive me for all that I have done to hurt you in the past and to tell you that I love you."

His partner was so surprised and convicted of his own sin that he responded by asking my friend to forgive him. Then, to my friend's surprise, his partner said, "I would like to become a Christian, too. Would you show me what I need to do?"

After my friend shared how to receive Christ as Savior and Lord, they knelt together to pray. Then they both came to tell me of this marvelous miracle of God's love in their lives and in their relationship.

Perhaps you have been in a similar situation and have wondered, "How can I really love that person?" No doubt you have found certain people hard to tolerate.

I encourage you to make a list of those whom you don't like and begin to love them by faith. Perhaps your boss, a fellow employee, your spouse, your children, or your father or mother are on the list. Confess any wrong attitudes you have about them to the Lord. Ask the Holy Spirit to fill you with Christ's love for each of them. Then seek to meet with them as you draw upon God's limitless, inexhaustible, overwhelming love for them by faith. Love every one of your "enemies" by faith—those who anger you, ignore you, bore you or frustrate you. Then, as God enables you, claiming the power of the Holy Spirit, go to the individuals with whom you have discord and conflict. Tell them you love them.

You will discover, as I have, that we can never run out of opportunities to love by faith. People are desperately waiting to be loved with God's love. And God has an unending supply of His divine, supernatural love for everyone. It is for us to claim, to grow on, to spread to others, and thus to reach everyone around us with the love that counts, the love that will bring them to Jesus Christ.

Bringing It All
Together

A very remarkable experience in my life took place in St. Louis, Missouri, years ago. I had finished my speaking engagements and rushed to the airport to catch a plane to Arrowhead Springs to be with Vonette and our sons, Zac and Brad. My travel schedule had been unusually busy so I had not spent as much time with them as I wanted and was especially eager to return home.

As I sped to the airport, I noticed storm clouds gathering rapidly. On arrival I rushed to the counter to purchase my ticket for the first plane leaving, only to find that all planes were grounded because of the weather.

Dismayed, I caught a bus back to the hotel. At first I was sad and terribly disappointed, but as I bumped along in the bus the Holy Spirit seemed to say, "I have something very important for you to do."

As I entered the hotel lobby, I joined other discouraged passengers waiting in line for rooms and struck up a conversation with one of them.

In the course of our conversation, he told me that he and his wife had been searching for God for the past two years. They had attended different churches every Sunday. But they had not found Him.

You can imagine my excitement and delight! I pulled a copy of the *Four Spiritual Laws* booklet from my pocket and used it as a tool to explain to him how he could know God in a personal way.

240

His response was enthusiastic; he was ready and eager to receive Christ. We found a quiet place and bowed together in prayer. As soon as we had finished praying, he asked, "What do you do for a living?"

When I explained that I had dedicated my life to telling others the Good News I had just shared with him, he responded with words I shall never forget: "Surely, you must bring a lot of happiness into this world!" With eyes filled with tears of gratitude, he asked if he could keep the *Four Spiritual Laws* booklet to share with his wife who was as hungry for God as he was. Of course I gladly gave it to him.

I went to bed that night with a joyful heart, singing praises to our wonderful Lord for allowing me to have the privilege of introducing this businessman to our Savior. As I went to sleep, his words played like an unbroken refrain in my mind: "You must bring a lot of happiness into this world."

For more than forty-five years I have had the joyful privilege of not only knowing Jesus Christ in a vital, personal way, but also of helping to share the Good News with millions of others around the world.

Perhaps you are on a spiritual journey like my friend in St. Louis. You may still be seeking to know God in a personal way.

If so, reading the next few pages may be the most important thing you do in your lifetime. Let me share four principles that, if applied, will enable you to know the reality of God in your life. And if you have already made the discovery of knowing Christ personally, may I encourage you to send a copy of this book to all your friends who are not believers.

1 *God loves you and created you to know Him personally.*

While the Bible is filled with assurances of God's love, perhaps the most telling verse is John 3:16:

> For God so loved the world, that He gave His only begotten Son, that whoever believes in Him should not perish, but have eternal life (NASB).

God not only loves each of us enough to give His only Son for us; He desires that we come to know Him personally:

> Now this is eternal life; that they may know you, the only true God, and Jesus Christ, whom you have sent (John 17:3, NIV).

What, then, prevents us from knowing God personally?

2 *Men and women are sinful and separated from God, so we cannot know Him personally or experience His love.*

We were all created to have fellowship with God, but because of our stubborn self-will, we chose to go our own independent way and fellowship with God was broken. This self-will, characterized by an attitude of active rebellion or passive indifference, is evidence of what the Bible calls sin.

> For all have sinned and fall short of the glory of God (Romans 3:23).

The Bible also tells us that "the wages of sin is death" (Romans 6:23), or spiritual separation from God. When we are in this state, a great gulf separates us from God because He cannot tolerate sin. People often try to bridge the gulf by doing good works or devoting themselves to religious or

New Age practices, but the Bible clearly teaches that there is only one way to bridge this gulf . . .

3 *Jesus Christ is God's ONLY provision for our sin. Through Him alone we can know God personally and experience His love.*

God's Word records three important facts to verify this principle: (1) Jesus Christ died in our place; (2) He rose from the dead; and (3) He is our only way to God:

> But God demonstrates His own love toward us, in that while we were yet sinners, Christ died for us (Romans 5:8, NASB).
>
> Christ died for our sins . . . He was buried . . . He was raised on the third day, according to the Scriptures . . . He appeared to Cephas, then to the twelve. After that He appeared to more than five hundred (1 Corinthians 15:3-6, NASB).
>
> Jesus said to him, "I am the way, and the truth, and the life; no one comes to the Father, but through Me" (John 14:6, NASB).

Thus, God has taken the loving initiative to bridge the gulf which separates us from Him by sending His Son, Jesus Christ, to die on the cross in our place to pay the penalty for our sin. But it is not enough just to know these truths . . .

4 *We must individually receive Jesus Christ as Savior and Lord; then we can know God personally and experience His love.*

John 1:12 records:

> But as many as received Him, to them He gave the right to become children of God, even to those who believe in His name (NASB).

243

What does it mean to "receive Christ"? The Scriptures tell us that we receive Christ through faith—not through "good works" or religious endeavors:

> For by grace you have been saved through faith; and that not of yourselves, it is the gift of God; not as a result of works, that no one should boast (Ephesians 2:8,9, NASB).

We are also told that receiving Christ means to personally invite Him into our lives:

> (Christ is speaking): Behold, I stand at the door and knock; if anyone hears My voice and opens the door, I will come in to him (Revelation 3:20, NASB).

Thus, receiving Christ involves turning to God from self ... and trusting Christ to come into our lives to forgive our sins and to make us the kind of people He wants us to be.

If you are not sure whether you have ever committed your life to Jesus Christ, I encourage you to do so—today! Here is a suggested prayer which has helped millions of men and women around the world express faith in Him and invite Him into their lives:

> Lord Jesus, I want to know You personally. Thank You for dying on the cross for my sins. I open the door of my life and receive You as my Savior and Lord. Thank You for forgiving my sins and giving me eternal life. Take control of the throne of my life. Make me the kind of person You want me to be.

If this prayer expresses the desire of your heart, why not pray it now? If you mean it sincerely, Jesus Christ will come into your life, just as He promised in Revelation 3:20. He keeps His promises! And there is another key promise I suggest you write indelibly in your mind:

> And the witness is this, that God has given us eternal life, and this life is in His Son. He who has the Son has the

life; he who does not have the Son of God does not have the life. These things I have written to you who believe in the name of the Son of God, in order that you may *know* that you have eternal life (1 John 5:11-13, NASB).

That's right—the man or woman who personally receives Christ as Savior and Lord is assured of everlasting life with Him in heaven. So, in summary, when you received Christ by faith, as an act of your will, many wonderful things happened including the following:

1. Christ came into your life (Revelation 3:20 and Colossians 1:27).

2. Your sins were forgiven (Colossians 1:14).

3. You became a child of God (John 1:12).

4. You received eternal life (John 5:24).

5. You began the great adventure for which God created you (John 10:10; 1 Thessalonians 5:18).

If you would like free literature to help you grow in your new walk with God, please write to me:

Bill Bright
Campus Crusade for Christ International
Arrowhead Springs, 45-00
San Bernardino, CA 92414

I would be delighted to send you Bible study materials that will help you understand your new relationship with God, understand His Word, the Bible, and enable you to start in your new life with Him.

Notes

Ted W. Engstrom
  1. New Life 2000 is a registered service mark of Campus Crusade for Christ Inc.

Robert H. Schuller
  1. From the song, "In the Garden," words and music by C. Austin Miles, © 1912 by Hall Mack Co.

* * *

I would like to thank the publishers for granting their authors permission to adapt material from the following books for use in this volume:

The God of Stones and Spiders by Charles Colson (Wheaton, IL: Crossway Books, 1990).

10 Years of God's Miracles by Paul Crouch (Santa Ana, California: ND).

The Gospel and the Briefcase by Ted DeMoss (Chattanooga, TN: Christian Business Men's Committee of USA, 1987).

Turning Hearts Toward Home by Rolf Zettersten (Irving, TX: Word Inc., 1989).

Sandy: A Heart for God by Leighton Ford (Downers Grove, IL: InterVarsity Press, 1985).

Worship His Majesty by Jack Hayford (Irving, TX: Word, Inc., 1987).

The Man in the Mirror and *I Surrender* by Pat Morley (Brentwood, TN: Wolgemuth and Hyatt, Inc., 1989 and 1990).

Say, "Yes!": How to Renew Your Spiritual Passion by Luis Palau (Portland, OR: Multnomah Press, 1991).

The Positive Power of Jesus Christ by Norman Vincent Peale (Wheaton, IL: Tyndale House Publishers, 1980).

Happy Trails by Roy Rogers and Dale Evans (Irving, TX: Word Inc., 1979).

Tough Times Never Last, But Tough People Do by Robert Schuller (Nashville, TN: Thomas Nelson Inc., 1983).